The UK
Ninja Foodi
Recipe Book with Colour Pictures

Delve into A Thorough Collection of Tasty & Easy-To-Follow Ninja Recipes in this Cookbook, Ensuring Quick and Convenient Meal Preparation

Pearl Engram

© Copyright 2024 – All rights reserved

This document is geared towards providing exact and reliable information with regards to the topic and issue covered. The publication is sold with the idea that the publisher is not required to render accounting, officially permitted, or otherwise, qualified services. If advice is necessary, legal, or professional, a practiced individual in the profession should be ordered. -From a Declaration of Principles which was accepted and approved equally by a Committee of the American Bar Association and a Committee of Publishers and Associations. In no way is it legal to reproduce, duplicate, or transmit any part of this document in either electronic means or in printed format. Recording of this publication is strictly prohibited and any storage of this document is not allowed unless with written permission from the publisher.

All rights reserved. The information provided herein is stated to be truthful and consistent, in that any liability, in terms of inattention or otherwise, by any usage or abuse of any policies, processes, or directions contained within is the solitary and utter responsibility of the recipient reader.

Under no circumstances will any legal responsibility or blame be held against the publisher for any reparation, damages, or monetary loss due to the information herein, either directly or indirectly. Respective authors own all copyrights not held by the publisher.

The information herein is offered for informational purposes solely, and is universal as so. The presentation of the information is without contract or any type of guarantee assurance. The trademarks that are used are without any consent, and the publication of the trademark is without permission or backing by the trademark owner.

All trademarks and brands within this book are for clarifying purposes only and are the owned by the owners themselves, not affiliated with this document.

·Contents·

01	Introduction	37	Chapter 4 Poultry Mains
02	What is Ninja Foodi?	45	Chapter 5 Seafood Mains
13	4-Week Meal Plan	53	Chapter 6 Beef, Pork, and Lamb
15	Chapter 1 Breakfast	61	Chapter 7 Desserts
22	Chapter 2 Vegetables and Sides	67	Conclusion
30	Chapter 3 Snacks and Appetisers	68	Appendix Recipes Index

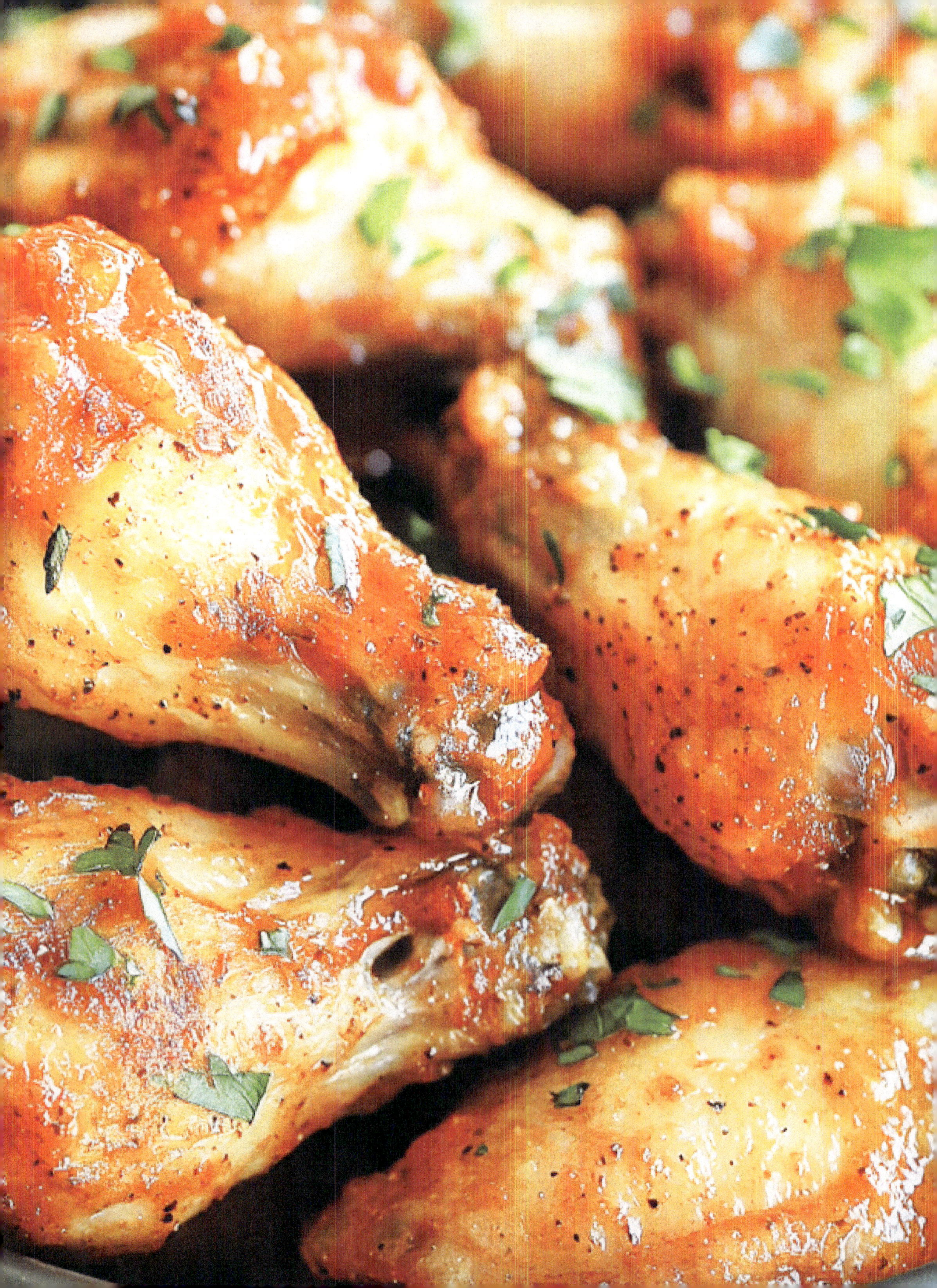

Introduction

Welcome to the Ninja Foodi Cookbook, your ultimate guide to mastering the Ninja Foodi Multi-Cooker. Whether you're a beginner looking to explore the world of multifunctional cooking or an experienced chef seeking to unlock the full potential of your kitchen arsenal, this cookbook is designed with you in mind.

Our goal is simple: We want to equip you with all the knowledge and skills needed to make the most of your Ninja Foodi. This versatile kitchen appliance is a game-changer, capable of Air Frying, broiling, baking/roasting, dehydrating, pressure cooking, steaming, slow cooking, making yoghurt, and searing/sautéing – all in one compact unit. It's a time-saving, space-saving wonder that simplifies your cooking routine.

Inside these pages, you'll find step-by-step instructions on using your Ninja Foodi effectively, ensuring your meals turn out perfectly every time. We'll also introduce you to various mouthwatering recipes showcasing the cooker's capabilities.

Whether you've just brought this culinary powerhouse into your kitchen or have had it for a while, our cookbook is your go-to resource. Get ready to discover the convenience, versatility, and efficiency of the Ninja Foodi. Let's embark on a delicious journey together and elevate your cooking game.

What is Ninja Foodi?

The Ninja Foodi is a remarkable kitchen companion that simplifies culinary adventures. It's like having multiple appliances rolled into one, making cooking a breeze for anyone, whether you're a beginner or an experienced chef.

Let's dive right in and explore what sets the Ninja Foodi apart.

Versatility at Its Best

Imagine having a kitchen appliance that can do it all. The Ninja Foodi boasts an impressive array of nine cooking functions, each tailored to create a wide range of dishes. This powerhouse does everything from Air Frying to grilling, baking/roasting, dehydrating, and even pressure cooking and steaming. You can even use it to slow cook, make yoghurt, and sear/sauté your ingredients perfectly.

Dual-Lid Design

One standout feature of the Ninja Foodi is its dual-lid design. It's like having a secret weapon in the kitchen. The pressure lid and crisping lid work harmoniously to give you the best of both worlds. You can easily switch between cooking functions, and after pressure cooking, crisp your food to perfection without any hassle.

Sizable Capacity

Cooking for a family or a gathering of friends? No problem! With a generous 7.5L capacity, the Ninja Foodi can easily handle your cooking needs.

Accessories Galore

It doesn't stop at the main unit. The Ninja Foodi has various parts and accessories, including a pressure lid, crisping lid, removable cooking pot, and Cook and crisp Basket.

User-Friendly

If you're worried about the complexity, fret not. The Ninja Foodi is designed with simplicity in mind. Its control panel features function buttons and operating buttons that are straightforward to use.

Safety First

Safety is paramount when it comes to kitchen appliances. The Ninja Foodi has several safety features, including a condensation collector, an anti-clog cap, and a pressure release valve. These features are there to ensure your cooking experience is convenient and safe.

Cooking Functions

The Ninja Foodi isn't just versatile; it's incredibly easy to use thanks to its intuitive operating buttons. Let's take a closer look at each of its nine cooking functions:

1. Air Fry: With this function, you can achieve the coveted crispy texture without excessive oil. Adjust the temperature, time, and start/stop buttons, and you're on your way to deliciously air-fried dishes.

2. Broil: Use high heat from above to caramelize and brown the tops of your food.

3. Bake/Roast: For perfectly baked or roasted dishes with a crispy exterior and tender interior, adjust the temperature, time, and start/stop buttons to suit your recipe.

4. Dehydrate: Preserve your favourite fruits and vegetables with the dehydrate function. It removes moisture, leaving you with tasty snacks for later.

5. Pressure Cook: Need a quick meal? The pressure cook function is your answer. Adjust the pressure level, time, and start/stop buttons to whip up delicious recipes quickly.

What is Ninja Foodi? | 03

6. Steam: Steam your way to nutritious and flavourful meals with the steam function. Set the time and start/stop, and your dishes will be ready to serve.

7. Slow Cook: The slow cook function is your best friend for tender and flavourful results. Adjust the temperature, time, and start/stop buttons.

8. Yoghurt: Make your own yoghurt at home and customize it to your heart's content. Adjust the temperature, time, and start/stop buttons to achieve the perfect consistency and flavour.

9. Sear/Sauté: Lock in flavour and create dishes with a crispy exterior using the sear/sauté function. Adjust the temperature, time, and start/stop buttons to your recipe's requirements.

10. Sous Vide: French for "under vacuum," this function slow cooks food sealed in a plastic bag in an accurately regulated water bath.

Operating Buttons

The Ninja Foodi not only offers versatility but also provides you with precise control over your cooking experience. Its intuitive operating buttons empower you to tailor your culinary creations accurately and confidently.

Smartlid Slider: As you move the slider, the available functions for each mode will illuminate.

DIAL: Once you've chosen a mode using the slider, use the dial to scroll through the available functions until your desired function is highlighted.

Temperature Adjustment:
The kitchen's perfect temperature is crucial, and the Ninja Foodi makes it a breeze. Use the temperature button to adjust the heat level according to your recipe's requirements. The START/STOP dial allows you to fine-tune the temperature precisely.

Time Control:
Timing is everything in cooking, and this cooker understands that. The time button lets you set the cooking duration, ensuring your dishes are perfectly cooked. With the START/STOP dial, you can easily adjust the time, giving you complete control over your cooking process.

Start/Stop Button:
This multifunctional button initiates the cooking process once you've configured your preferred settings. It's as simple as pressing the button to kickstart your culinary journey. If needed, pressing it again during cooking will halt the current function.

The Ninja Foodi is a kitchen marvel that combines versatility, user-friendliness, and safety features. Its nine cooking functions and intuitive operating buttons make it a perfect addition to any kitchen, making cooking a joy for everyone, from beginners to seasoned chefs.

Benefits of Using It

Using the Ninja Foodi isn't just about cooking; it's about transforming your kitchen experience you never thought possible. Let's delve into the benefits of this versatile kitchen appliance to your cooking journey.

Versatility Beyond Compare

The Ninja Foodi has nine cooking functions, allowing you to create many dishes. From Air Frying to steaming, baking/roasting to pressure cooking. This versatility means you can regularly explore new culinary horizons and surprise your taste buds.

Convenience Redefined

Cooking for a family or a group of friends has never been this hassle-free. With a spacious 7.5L volume, the Ninja Foodi eliminates the need for multiple pots and pans. Its user-friendly control panel, adorned with function and operating buttons, ensures effortless operation. We'll go through each of them in the upcoming section.

Time-Saving Magic

In today's fast-paced world, time is of the essence, and the Ninja Foodi understands that. Performing multiple cooking functions streamlines your kitchen routine. You can whip up delectable dishes without spending endless hours in the kitchen.

Healthier Cooking Choices

Craving crispy food without the guilt? The Ninja Foodi's Air Fry function allows you to air fry your favourite dishes to crispy perfection, all without drowning them in oil. It's a game-changer for anyone conscious of their dietary choices.

Safety as a Priority

Your safety is paramount, and the Ninja Foodi doesn't compromise. With a range of safety features, including a condensation collector, anti-clog cap, and pressure release valve, you can cook with confidence.

Save Space, Cook Big

The Ninja Foodi is your space-saving hero. It's a single, compact unit that replaces multiple kitchen appliances. There is no need for a crowded countertop; the Ninja Foodi brings simplicity and efficiency to your kitchen.

Endless Culinary Adventures

With twelve cooking functions at your disposal, your culinary adventures know no bounds. From savoury to sweet, the Ninja Foodi empowers you to create various dishes. Experiment with recipes, and impress your family and friends.

Perfect Results, Every Time

Precision is vital in cooking, and the Ninja Foodi delivers. Its intuitive operating buttons allow you to set the perfect recipe temperature and time. No more guesswork; your dishes come out consistently delicious.

A Healthier You, a Healthier Planet

By choosing the Ninja Foodi, you're making healthier cooking choices and contributing to a healthier planet. Its energy-efficient design means less power consumption, reducing your carbon footprint.

In conclusion, the Ninja Foodi isn't just an appliance; it's a game-changer. Its versatility, convenience, time-saving capabilities, and commitment to healthier cooking make it an indispensable tool in any kitchen. It's time to elevate your cooking game and savour the benefits of the Ninja Foodi.

Step-By-Step Using It

Welcome to the heart of your culinary journey, where we'll unravel the secrets of using the Ninja Foodi step by step. It's a kitchen wizard, and you're about to become its master.

Getting Acquainted with the Control Panel

The Ninja Foodi's control panel is your command centre. Here's a quick tour:

Function Buttons: These allow you to select your cooking function. Press the button and use the START/STOP dial to choose your desired mode.

Operating Buttons: The "Temp" button lets you tweak the cooking temperature and pressure level. Use the START/STOP dial for fine adjustments. The "Time" button sets the cooking time, again adjusted with the dial. Press the "Start/Stop" button to kickstart cooking and stop it mid-way if needed. The "Power" button shuts down the unit and all cooking modes.

Setting Up for Success

Before diving into cooking, ensure a safe setup:

1. Stable Surface: Place your Ninja Foodi on a clean, dry, and stable surface. Keep it away from hot surfaces, gas or electric burners, and heated ovens.

2. Plug It In: Plug the power cord into a grounded electrical outlet.

3. Position It Right: Position the appliance away from walls and cabinets during use to prevent steam damage.

4. Safety Checks: Inspect the pressure release valve and red float valve before cooking for any clogs or obstructions. Clean them if necessary, and ensure the red float valve moves freely.

5. Shield Yourself: Always tilt the lid between your body and the inner pot, protecting you from steam and hot liquids.

6. Use Recommended Attachments: Use SharkNinja Silicone rings only. Ensure the silicone ring is installed correctly and the lid is securely closed before operation. Replace the silicone ring if it's torn or damaged.

7. Mind the Food: Certain foods, like apple sauce, cranberries, barley, oatmeal, or other cereals, can foam, froth, and splutter during pressure cooking, clogging the pressure release valve. Avoid pressure cooking these foods unless you're following a Ninja Foodi recipe.

8. Follow Instructions: Adhere to the maximum and minimum quantities of liquid as stated in instructions and recipes.

9. Safety First: Utilize protective hot pads or insulated oven mitts when handling the appliance during and after operation.

Cooking Functions

Now that you're all set up let's dive into the exciting

world of Ninja Foodi cooking. Whether you're air-crisping, grilling, or slow cooking, we've got you covered.

Air Fry:
1. Select the "Air Fry" function on the control panel.
2. Adjust the temperature and time using the "Temp" and "Time" buttons.
3. Press the "Start/Stop" button to commence cooking.

Broil:
1. Move slider to AIR FRY/STOVETOP, then use the dial to select BROIL.
2. There is no temperature adjustment available or necessary when using the Broil function.
3. Use the up and down arrows to the right of the display to adjust the cook time in minute increments up to 30 minutes.
4. Press START/STOP to begin cooking.
5. When cook time reaches zero, the unit will beep and "End" will flash 3 times on the display.

Bake/Roast:
1. Opt for the "Bake/Roast" function on the control panel.
2. Adjust the temperature and time using the "Temp" and "Time" buttons.
3. Press the "Start/Stop" button to start cooking.

Dehydrate:
1. Select the "Dehydrate" function on the control panel.
2. Adjust the temperature and time using the "Temp" and "Time" buttons.
3. Press the "Start/Stop" button to begin the dehydrating process.

Pressure Cook:
1. Add your ingredients and the required liquid to the cooking pot.
2. Select the "Pressure Cook" function on the control panel.
3. Adjust the pressure level, temperature, and time using the "Temp" and "Time" buttons.
4. Ensure the pressure release valve is in the SEAL position.
5. Press the "Start/Stop" button to commence pressure cooking.

Steam:
1. Place your food and liquid in the cooking pot.
2. Opt for the "Steam" function on the control panel.
3. Adjust the temperature and time using the "Temp" and "Time" buttons.
4. Ensure the pressure release valve is in the SEAL

position.
5. Press the "Start/Stop" button to start steaming.

Slow Cook:
1. Add your ingredients and liquid to the cooking pot.
2. Select the "Slow Cook" function on the control panel.
3. Adjust the temperature and time using the "Temp" and "Time" buttons.
4. Press the "Start/Stop" button to begin slow cooking.

Yoghurt:
1. Pour milk into the cooking pot.
2. Choose the "Yoghurt" function on the control panel.
3. Adjust the temperature and time using the "Temp" and "Time" buttons.
4. Press the "Start/Stop" button to make yoghurt.

Sear/Sauté:
1. Select the "Sear/Sauté" function on the control panel.
2. Adjust the temperature and time using the "Temp" and "Time" buttons.
3. Press the "Start/Stop" button to begin searing or sautéing.

With these steps, you can wield the Ninja Foodi for various culinary adventures at your fingertips.

Tips and Tricks

Now that you're on your way to becoming a Ninja Foodi expert let's delve into some tips, tricks, and recommendations to elevate your cooking game:

1. Liquid Precision: Always stick to the recommended liquid quantity for each recipe. Too little liquid can lead to burning, while excessive liquid can result in watery dishes.

2. Preheating: Kickstart your cooking by preheating the appliance. This ensures even cooking and superior results.

3. Function Know-How: Each cooking function has a specific purpose. Use the correct function for your dish.

4. Seasoning Sensation: Enhance flavours by seasoning your food before cooking. Incorporate herbs, spices, and marinades to elevate your creations.

5. Arrangement Art: Arrange food evenly in the cooking pot without overlapping for consistent results. Use parchment paper or foil pouches for smaller ingredients.

6. Watch and Adjust: Keep an eye on your dish's progress. Adjust temperature and time as needed to perfect your creation.

7. Crisping Magic: The crisping lid adds a crispy touch to your food. Ensure you use it at the recommended cooking time and temperature.

8. Pressure Release Caution: When releasing pressure, follow instructions meticulously and keep your face and hands away from steam.

9. Rest for Excellence: Allow your cooked food to rest for a few minutes. This helps flavours develop and enhances tenderness.

By implementing these tips, your Ninja Foodi creations will shine.

Safety Precautions

While culinary adventures are exciting, safety is paramount. Follow these precautions:

1. Pressure Release: When releasing pressure, ensure the pressure release valve is set to VENT. Keep your face and hands clear of the steam, using a long-handled utensil to turn the valve.

2. Lid Handling: When opening the lid, keep your face away from the lid to prevent steam burns. Use oven mitts or a towel to protect your hands.

3. Handling Hot Food: Shield your hands with oven mitts or insulated gloves when handling hot food. Allow it to cool briefly before touching.

4. Cleaning Caution: Unplug the appliance and let it cool before cleaning. Use a soft cloth and avoid submerging the appliance in water or other liquids.

5. Safety Features: The appliance has safety features, including a condensation collector, anti-clog cap, and pressure release valve, ensuring safe and efficient usage.

Following these precautions will make your Ninja Foodi journey exciting and secure.

This comprehensive guide prepares you to embark on a culinary journey with your Ninja Foodi. From setup to achieving mouthwatering results, you've got the tools and knowledge to create delectable dishes. So, what will you cook first?

Tips for Using Accessories

Unlock the full potential of your culinary adventures with the Ninja Foodi by mastering the art of using accessories. Here are some invaluable tips to enhance your cooking experience:

1. Choose the Right Tool: Ninja offers many accessories tailor-made for the Ninja Foodi. Ensure you select the accessory that perfectly complements your cooking endeavour. Each accessory is designed with a specific function, so picking the right one is key to culinary success.

2. Harness the Power of Silicone: The silicone ring and rack are indispensable companions when pressure cooking. Remember to clean them regularly to maintain hygiene, and if you notice any damage to the silicone ring, don't hesitate to replace it for continued safety and performance.

3. Specialized Tins for Baking Delights: The loaf and multi-purpose tin create delectable bread, casseroles, dips, and sweet and savoury pies. Just adhere to the recommended cooking time and temperature for delicious results.

4. Skewer Stand Extravaganza: If you own a 7.5L model, don't miss out on the skewer stand's capabilities. It's your ticket to crafting mouthwatering kebabs. The package even includes 15 skewers, so you can get creative with your culinary creations.

5. Maintenance for Peak Performance: Regularly clean your accessories to ensure they deliver top-notch performance. A simple wipe with a soft cloth will suffice. Avoid immersing them in water or other liquids to prolong their lifespan and keep your culinary adventures in full swing.

With these expert tips and creativity, you'll elevate your cooking game and make the most of your Ninja Foodi accessories.

Straight from The Store

Congratulations on your new Ninja Foodi! As you unpack this versatile kitchen marvel, here are some essential steps to ensure a smooth transition from the store to your kitchen:

1. Unpacking and Inspection: Begin by carefully unpacking the appliance and removing all packaging materials. Take a moment to inspect each component to ensure that nothing has been damaged during transportation. Verify that all parts and accessories are present and in excellent condition.

2. Read the Instruction Manual: Before you start cooking, take the time to read the instruction manual thoroughly.

3. Wash and Dry: Wash the cooking pot, pressure lid, and any included accessories with warm soapy water. Ensure that they are clean and free from any manufacturing residues. After washing, dry them thoroughly to prevent water droplets during cooking.

4. Accessories Installation: Follow the instructions in the manual to install the condensation collector and anti-clog cap.

5. Setup and Positioning: Position your Ninja Foodi on a stable and level surface. Ensure it's placed away from walls and cabinets to prevent any potential steam damage. Plug the appliance into a grounded electrical outlet to power it up.

6. Control Panel Familiarization: Take a moment to acquaint yourself with the control panel and its cooking functions.

7. Test Cycle: Running a test cycle is a good practice before embarking on your culinary journey. Refer to the instruction manual for guidance on performing the test cycle.

8. Ready to Cook: Once the test cycle is complete and you're confident in the appliance's functionality, your Ninja Foodi is ready to transform your kitchen experiences.

These steps will effectively set up your Ninja Foodi and ensure a safe and enjoyable cooking journey.

Cleaning and Caring for Your Ninja Foodi

Properly maintaining your Ninja Foodi is essential to keep it in peak condition and ensure years of culinary excellence. Here's a comprehensive guide to cleaning and caring for your appliance:

1. Unplug Before You Clean: Always disconnect your Ninja Foodi from the wall socket before cleaning or maintenance.

2. Wipe Down the Exterior: A simple wipe with a damp

cloth will do the trick for the cooker base and control panel. This helps maintain the appliance's sleek appearance.

3. Dishwasher-Friendly Parts: The cooking pot, silicone ring, reversible rack, Cook & Crisp Basket, and detachable diffuser are dishwasher-safe. Feel free to place these parts in your dishwasher for a hassle-free clean-up.

4. Hand Wash with Care: Some components, like the pressure release valve and anti-clog cap, prefer a gentle hand wash with water and mild dish soap. These small yet vital parts should be kept squeaky clean.

5. Caring for the Unit Lid: A quick wipe with a wet cloth or paper towel will remove any lingering residue after the crisping lid cools down. This ensures your unit lid stays in top shape.

6. Dealing with Stubborn Residue: If you encounter stubborn food residue on the cooking pot, reversible rack, or Cook & Crisp Basket, don't use scouring pads. Instead, soak the affected part in water before cleaning. Use a non-abrasive cleanser or liquid dish soap and a gentle nylon pad or brush for tougher spots.

7. Air-Dry All Parts: After cleaning the various components, air-dry them thoroughly after each use. Proper drying helps prevent any unwanted odours or moisture buildup.

8. Silicone Ring Care: The silicone ring is crucial for maintaining a proper seal. To remove it, gently pull it outward, section by section, from the silicone ring rack. The ring can be installed with either side facing up. When reinstalling it, press it down into the rack section by section.

9. Odor Management: Remove any food debris and the anti-clog cap after each use to keep your silicone ring odour-free. Wash it with warm, soapy water or toss it in the dishwasher. Please note that it may absorb the aroma of certain acidic foods. Consider having more than one silicone ring on hand for different dishes.

10. Handle with Care: Always exercise caution when dealing with the silicone ring. Avoid excessive force, as this can lead to deformation and affect its pressure-sealing capabilities.

By adhering to these cleaning and maintenance guidelines, you can extend the life of your Ninja Foodi, ensuring it remains a reliable kitchen companion for countless meals to come.

Frequently Asked Questions & Notes

As you embark on your culinary journey with the Ninja Foodi, you may have questions and considerations. This section answers some frequently asked questions (FAQ) and essential notes to ensure your cooking experience is smooth and enjoyable.

Frequently Asked Questions (FAQ)

1. What is a multi-cooker, and how does it work?
A multi-cooker is a versatile kitchen appliance that combines various cooking methods, such as pressure cooking, slow cooking, air frying, and more, in a single device. It works by using different settings and accessories to perform these cooking functions.

2. Is the Ninja Foodi suitable for beginners?
Yes, the Ninja Foodi is designed with user-friendliness in mind and comes with clear instructions. It's suitable for both beginners and experienced cooks.

3. What is the difference between slow cooking and pressure cooking?
Slow cooking involves cooking food at low temperatures over an extended period, resulting in tender dishes. On the other hand, pressure cooking uses steam pressure to cook food quickly, reducing cooking times significantly.

4. Can I use metal utensils with the Ninja Foodi?
It's advisable to use utensils made of non-abrasive materials like silicone or wood to avoid damaging the non-stick coating of the cooking pot.

5. Can I cook frozen food directly in the Ninja Foodi?
You can cook frozen food, but it may require slight cooking times and temperature adjustments. Always follow recommended guidelines and monitor the cooking process.

Notes

1. Recipe Adaptation: Feel free to experiment with your favourite recipes and adapt them to the Ninja Foodi's cooking functions. It's a versatile appliance that can handle various dishes.

2. Steam Release Safety: Always exercise caution when releasing steam from the pressure cooker. Keep your hands and face away from the steam valve to prevent burns.

3. Silicone Ring Maintenance: Regularly clean and inspect the silicone ring for any signs of wear or damage. Replace it if necessary to maintain a proper seal.

4. Temperature and Time Adjustments: Adjust cooking temperatures and times based on your preferences and the specific requirements of your recipes.

5. Food Quantity Consideration: Be mindful of minimum and maximum food quantities when using the appliance to achieve the best results.

With these FAQs and notes in mind, you can make the most of your Ninja Foodi. Enjoy your culinary adventures!

4-Week Meal Plan

Week 1

Day 1:
Breakfast: Chocolate Almond Rolls
Lunch: Garlic Brown Mushrooms
Snack: Olive-Stuffed Jalapeños
Dinner: Flavourful Beef with Carrots
Dessert: Chocolate Mug Cake

Day 2:
Breakfast: Spinach Artichoke Pizza
Lunch: Mashed Cauliflower Soup
Snack: Barbecue Beef Meatballs
Dinner: Potato Salmon Fish Cakes
Dessert: Molten Lava Cake

Day 3:
Breakfast: Parmesan Garlic Bread
Lunch: Tomato & Ricotta Cheese Risotto
Snack: Party Chex Nuts Snack
Dinner: Lamb and Wheat Berries Stew
Dessert: Butter Cake

Day 4:
Breakfast: Raspberry Yoghurt Parfait
Lunch: Air Fried Bell Peppers
Snack: Pepperoni Pizza Bombs with Marinara Sauce
Dinner: Chicken Fajita Rollups
Dessert: Nutty Fruitcake

Day 5:
Breakfast: Bacon and Egg Fried Rice
Lunch: BBQ Beef Cheeseburgers
Snack: Classic Deviled Eggs
Dinner: Savoury Rump Roast
Dessert: Zesty Raspberry Muffins

Day 6:
Breakfast: Blueberry Bread Pudding
Lunch: Spicy Potato Chunks
Snack: Parmesan Breaded Aubergine Slices
Dinner: Spiced Fish Tacos
Dessert: Pumpkin Pudding

Day 7:
Breakfast: Blueberry Muffins
Lunch: Indian Style Spaghetti Squash
Snack: Cheese Chicken Meatballs
Dinner: Crisp Chicken Tenders
Dessert: Chocolate Chip Cookies

Week 2

Day 1:
Breakfast: Coconut Pecan Steel-Cut Oats
Lunch: Potato, Tomato and Cauliflower Curry
Snack: Savoury Buffalo Chicken Wings
Dinner: Turkey Bolognese with Spaghetti Squash
Dessert: Sugared Dough Dippers with Chocolate Sauce

Day 2:
Breakfast: Sweet Bacon Knots
Lunch: Flavourful Sweet-Sour Red Cabbage
Snack: Cheese Cauliflower Pizza Crusts
Dinner: Lemony Lamb with Chickpea & Pitas
Dessert: Egg Custard

Day 3:
Breakfast: Coconut Mango Steel-Cut Oats
Lunch: Roasted Vegetable Bowls
Snack: Loaded Baby Potatoes
Dinner: Herb-Garlic Fillet Mignon
Dessert: Pumpkin Pudding

Day 4:
Breakfast: Bacon & Sweet Potatoes Stew
Lunch: Crispy Sweet Potatoes
Snack: Olive-Stuffed Jalapeños
Dinner: Chicken Thighs & Quinoa Bowls
Dessert: Butter Cake

Day 5:
Breakfast: Chocolate Almond Rolls
Lunch: Mashed Potatoes with Kale
Snack: Easy Air-Fried Pumpkin Seeds
Dinner: Turkey Breast with Mustard-Maple Glaze
Dessert: Zesty Raspberry Muffins

Day 6:
Breakfast: Parmesan Garlic Bread
Lunch: Collard Greens with Bacon
Snack: Chicken Wings with Barbecue Sauce
Dinner: BBQ Beef Brisket
Dessert: Nutty Fruitcake

Day 7:
Breakfast: Apple Walnut Muffins
Lunch: Freekeh-Aubergine Bowls
Snack: Classic Deviled Eggs
Dinner: Cider & Mustard–Braised Chicken Thighs
Dessert: Peach Crumble

Week 3

Day 1:
Breakfast: Raspberry Yoghurt Parfait
Lunch: Spicy Potato Chunks
Snack: Pepperoni Pizza Bombs with Marinara Sauce
Dinner: Pork Chops with Bacon & Cream Sauce
Dessert: Chocolate Chip Cookies

Day 2:
Breakfast: Blueberry Bread Pudding
Lunch: Mashed Cauliflower Soup
Snack: Parmesan Breaded Aubergine Slices
Dinner: Lemon Cajun Salmon
Dessert: Chocolate Mug Cake

Day 3:
Breakfast: Bacon and Egg Fried Rice
Lunch: Garlic Brown Mushrooms
Snack: Cheese Chicken Meatballs
Dinner: Crispy Oats Crusted Chicken Drumsticks
Dessert: Molten Lava Cake

Day 4:
Breakfast: Coconut Mango Steel-Cut Oats
Lunch: Air Fried Bell Peppers
Snack: Olive-Stuffed Jalapeños
Dinner: Beef Pot with Potatoes and Carrots
Dessert: Butter Cake

Day 5:
Breakfast: Blueberry Muffins
Lunch: Tomato & Ricotta Cheese Risotto
Snack: Cheese Cauliflower Pizza Crusts
Dinner: Honey-Soy Braised Salmon
Dessert: Egg Custard

Day 6:
Breakfast: Spinach Artichoke Pizza
Lunch: Crispy Sweet Potatoes
Snack: Party Chex Nuts Snack
Dinner: Delicious Chicken Mushroom Kabobs
Dessert: Pumpkin Pudding

Day 7:
Breakfast: Bacon & Sweet Potatoes Stew
Lunch: Collard Greens with Bacon
Snack: Barbecue Beef Meatballs
Dinner: Pulled Turkey
Dessert: Nutty Fruitcake

Week 4

Day 1:
Breakfast: Chocolate Almond Rolls
Lunch: Mashed Potatoes with Kale
Snack: Savoury Buffalo Chicken Wings
Dinner: Coconut Shrimp
Dessert: Peach Crumble

Day 2:
Breakfast: Apple Walnut Muffins
Lunch: Roasted Broccoli
Snack: Chicken Wings with Barbecue Sauce
Dinner: Juicy Chicken Thighs
Dessert: Molten Lava Cake

Day 3:
Breakfast: Coconut Pecan Steel-Cut Oats
Lunch: Indian Style Spaghetti Squash
Snack: Loaded Baby Potatoes
Dinner: Roasted Salmon with Capers-Yogurt Dressing
Dessert: Chocolate Mug Cake

Day 4:
Breakfast: Parmesan Garlic Bread
Lunch: Freekeh-Aubergine Bowls
Snack: Pepperoni Pizza Bombs with Marinara Sauce
Dinner: Prawns and Ear Corn Boil
Dessert: Zesty Raspberry Muffins

Day 5:
Breakfast: Sweet Bacon Knots
Lunch: Flavourful Sweet-Sour Red Cabbage
Snack: Easy Air-Fried Pumpkin Seeds
Dinner: Chicken & Ziti Casserole
Dessert: Chocolate Chip Cookies

Day 6:
Breakfast: Bacon & Sweet Potatoes Stew
Lunch: Potato, Tomato and Cauliflower Curry
Snack: Cheese Cauliflower Pizza Crusts
Dinner: Parmesan Tilapia Fillets
Dessert: Sugared Dough Dippers with Chocolate Sauce

Day 7:
Breakfast: Coconut Mango Steel-Cut Oats
Lunch: Roasted Vegetable Bowls
Snack: Classic Deviled Eggs
Dinner: London Broil with Garlic Butter
Dessert: Egg Custard

Chapter 1 Breakfast

16	Apple Walnut Muffins	19	Bacon and Egg Fried Rice
16	Spinach Artichoke Pizza	19	Parmesan Garlic Bread
17	Coconut Mango Steel–Cut Oats	20	Blueberry Bread Pudding
17	Chocolate Almond Rolls	20	Bacon & Sweet Potatoes Stew
18	Raspberry Yoghurt Parfait	21	Blueberry Muffins
18	Coconut Pecan Steel–Cut Oats	21	Sweet Bacon Knots

Apple Walnut Muffins

⏱ **Prep Time: 10 minutes**   🍳 **Cook: 11 minutes**   ◆ **Serves: 8**

120g flour
125g sugar
1 teaspoon baking powder
¼ teaspoon baking soda
¼ teaspoon salt
1 teaspoon cinnamon
¼ teaspoon ginger
¼ teaspoon nutmeg
1 egg
4 tablespoons pancake syrup
4 tablespoons melted butter
40g unsweetened applesauce
½ teaspoon vanilla extract
30g chopped walnuts
30g diced apple

1. In a suitable bowl, stir flour, sugar, baking soda, baking powder, salt, cinnamon, ginger, and nutmeg. 2. In a suitable bowl, beat egg until frothy. Add syrup, butter, applesauce, and vanilla and mix well. 3. Place the Cook & Crisp Basket in your Pressure Cooker Steam Fryer. 4. Pour the prepared egg mixture into dry recipe ingredients and stir just until moistened. 5. Gently stir in nuts and diced apple. 6. Divide batter among the 8 muffin cups. 7. Place 4 muffin cups in "cook & crisp basket". 8. Put on the Smart Lid on top of the Ninja Foodi Steam Fryer. 9. Move the Lid Slider to the "Air Fry/Stovetop". Select the "Air Fry" mode for cooking. 10. Air fry at 165°C for around 9 to 11 minutes. 11. Repeat with remaining 4 muffins or until toothpick inserted in centre comes out clean.

Per serving: Calories: 289; Fat: 14g; Sodium: 791mg; Carbs: 8.9g; Fibre: 4.6g; Sugar 8g; Protein 16g

Spinach Artichoke Pizza

⏱ **Prep Time: 10 minutes**   🍳 **Cook: 18 minutes**   ◆ **Serves: 2**

2 tablespoons olive oil
90g fresh spinach
2 cloves garlic, minced
1 (230g) pizza dough ball
60g grated mozzarella cheese
55g grated Fontina cheese
65g artichoke hearts, chopped
2 tablespoons grated Parmesan cheese
¼ teaspoon dried oregano
Salt and black pepper, to taste

1. Heat the oil in a suitable sauté pan on the stovetop. Add the spinach and half of the garlic to the pan, sautéing for a few minutes until the spinach wilts, then transfer it to a bowl. 2. Place the Cook & Crisp Basket in your Pressure Cooker Steam Fryer. 3. Line the Ninja Foodi Pressure Steam Fryer basket with aluminium. Brush the foil with oil. Shape the prepared dough into a circle and place it on top of the foil. 4. Brush the prepared dough with olive oil and transfer it into the Ninja Foodi Pressure Steam Fryer basket with the foil on the bottom. 5. Put on the Smart Lid on top of the Ninja Foodi Steam Fryer. 6. Move the Lid Slider to the "Air Fry/Stovetop". Cook the prepared pizza dough on "Air Fry" mode at 200°C for around 6 minutes. 7. Flip the prepared dough, remove the aluminium foil, and brush it with olive oil again. Air-fry for 4 minutes. 8. Add the mozzarella and Fontina cheeses over the prepared dough. Spread the spinach and artichoke hearts over the dough. Sprinkle with Parmesan cheese and dried oregano, then drizzle with olive oil. Put on the Smart Lid on top of the Ninja Foodi Steam Fryer. Move the Lid Slider to the "Air Fry/Stovetop". Cook on "Air Fry" mode at 175°C for around 8 minutes, until the cheese has melted and is browned. 9. Serve.

Per serving: Calories: 372; Fat: 20g; Sodium: 891mg; Carbs: 29g; Fibre: 3g; Sugar 8g; Protein 17g

Coconut Mango Steel-Cut Oats

⏰ **Prep Time: 25 minutes** 🍳 **Cook: 15 minutes** 🍽 **Serves: 4**

1 (385g) can coconut milk
220g steel-cut oats
Salt
45g to 65g loosely packed coconut sugar or brown sugar
1 large mango, pitted, peeled, and diced
25g unsweetened coconut flakes, lightly toasted
30g chopped macadamia nuts

1. Combine the coconut milk, 300ml warm water, the oats, 01and a generous pinch of salt in the pot. 2. Close the lid, turn the pressure release valve to SEAL position, and then move the slider to PRESSURE. Select HI and set the cooking time to 13 minutes. Press START/STOP to begin cooking. When finished, release the pressure naturally. 3. Stir the sugar into the oats. The oats will thicken a bit upon standing. 4. Top the oats with the mango, coconut flakes, and nuts. Serve warm.

Per Serving: Calories 275; Fat: 11.91g; Sodium: 178mg; Carbs: 48.69g; Fibre: 8.8g; Sugar: 24.94g; Protein: 7.49g

Chocolate Almond Rolls

⏰ **Prep Time: 10 minutes** 🍳 **Cook: 8 minutes** 🍽 **Serves: 6**

1 (230g) tube of crescent roll dough
160g semi-sweet or bittersweet chocolate chunks
1 egg white, beaten
25g sliced almonds
Powdered sugar, for dusting
Butter or oil

1. Unwrap the thawed crescent roll dough and separate it into triangles with the points facing away from you. Place a row of chocolate chunks along the bottom edge of the prepared dough. 2. Roll the prepared dough up around the chocolate and then place another row of chunks on the prepared dough. Roll again and finish with one or two chocolate chunks. Be sure to leave the end free of chocolate so that it can adhere to the rest of the roll. 3. Brush the tops of the crescent rolls with the beaten egg white and sprinkle the almonds on top, pressing them into the crescent dough so they adhere. 4. Place the Cook & Crisp Basket in your Pressure Cooker Steam Fryer. 5. Brush the bottom of the Ninja Foodi Pressure Steam Fryer basket with butter or oil and transfer the crescent rolls to the basket. 6. Put on the Smart Lid on top of the Ninja Foodi Steam Fryer. 7. Move the Lid Slider to the "Air Fry/Stovetop". Select the "Air Fry" mode for cooking. 8. Air-fry rolls at 175°C for 8 minutes. 9. Remove and let the crescent rolls cool before dusting with powdered sugar and serving.

Per serving: Calories: 372; Fat: 20g; Sodium: 891mg; Carbs: 29g; Fibre: 3g; Sugar 8g; Protein 17g

Chapter 1 Breakfast | 17

Raspberry Yoghurt Parfait

⏰ Prep Time: 30 minutes   🍲 Cook: 8 hours   ❖ Serves: 4

For the yogurt
1920ml whole milk or 2% milk
2 tablespoons plain yogurt with live active cultures
For the parfaits
45g packed brown sugar
1 vanilla bean
120g fresh raspberries
10g freeze-dried raspberries, crushed

1. Pour the milk into the pot and lock on the lid. Move slider to AIR FRY/STOVETOP and use the dial to select YOGURT. Select "FEr" and adjust the cooking time to 8 hours. Press START/STOP to begin pasteurization. Unit will display "boiL" while pasteurizing. 2. When pasteurization temperature is reached, the unit will beep and display "COOL." Once the milk has cooled to 45°C, open the lid and skim the top of the milk. Add active cultures to milk and stir to combine. Close the lid and press START/STOP to begin incubation process. 3. When the cooking time is up, pour the yogurt into clean containers and store in the refrigerator for 8 hours before serving so the yogurt can continue to thicken. The yogurt can be refrigerated and stored for up to 7 days. 4. In a medium bowl, Whisk together 900g of the yogurt and the brown sugar in a medium bowl. Slice the vanilla bean lengthwise with a sharp paring knife, then use the dull side of the knife to scrape the sticky black vanilla seeds into the yogurt. Whisk to combine. 5. Spoon half the yogurt into four 1-cup sundae glasses or other serving dishes. Top the dish with the fresh raspberries and then the remaining yogurt. Sprinkle the dish with the freeze-dried berries and serve.

Per Serving: Calories 557; Fat: 15.35g; Sodium: 225mg; Carbs: 92.12g; Fibre: 2.2g; Sugar: 89.2g; Protein: 15.42g

Coconut Pecan Steel-Cut Oats

⏰ Prep Time: 15 minutes   🍲 Cook: 5 minutes   ❖ Serves: 4

320g steel-cut oats
710ml water
400ml can full-fat coconut milk, divided
80ml pure maple syrup, plus more to taste
½ tsp. sea salt
55g toasted pecan pieces
2 tsp. (5g) ground cinnamon (optional)

1. Combine the oats, water, 240ml of the coconut milk, and the maple syrup and salt in the pot, and then give the mixture a quick stir. 2. Close the lid, turn the pressure release valve to SEAL position, and then move the slider to PRESSURE. Select HI and set the cooking time to 4 minutes. Press START/STOP to begin cooking. When finished, release the pressure naturally. 3. Remove the lid, and stir in the remaining coconut milk and additional maple syrup to taste. 4. Serve with the toasted pecans and sprinkle with the cinnamon (if using).

Per Serving: Calories 581; Fat: 38.52g; Sodium: 3228mg; Carbs: 77.65g; Fibre: 15.8g; Sugar: 20.63g; Protein: 17.33g

Bacon and Egg Fried Rice

⏰ **Prep Time:** 15 minutes 🍱 **Cook:** 30 minutes ❖ **Serves:** 4-6

295ml water
190g uncooked brown rice
Salt
1 tsp. sesame oil
5 slices raw bacon, chopped
1 tsp. soy sauce
3 large eggs, beaten
65g frozen peas
Freshly ground black pepper
Sriracha sauce, for topping (optional)
4 green onions, sliced

1. Combine the water, rice and a pinch of salt in the pot. 2. Close the lid, turn the pressure release valve to SEAL position, and then move the slider to PRESSURE. Select HI and set the cooking time to 15 minutes. Press START/STOP to begin cooking. When finished, release the pressure naturally. 3. Use a fork to fluff the rice, and then transfer it to a large plate. Set aside.
4. Clean out the pot and then return it to the unit. 5. Select SEAR/SAUTÉ mode, and adjust the cooking temperature to Lo3. 6. When the pot is hot, add sesame oil and chopped bacon, and sauté them for 5 to 7 minutes until each piece is crispy; stir in the soy sauce, then push the bacon to one side of the pot; add the eggs to the opposite side of the pot, and gently push the eggs back and forth until they start to scramble slightly. Add the cooked rice and quickly mix everything together. 7. Stop the process and stir in the peas. Let the fried rice sit for a minute or two until the peas have thawed and warmed. 8. Season the dish with salt and pepper to taste, and top with sriracha sauce (if using) and the green onions. 9. Serve and enjoy.

Per Serving: Calories 258; Fat: 12.8g; Sodium: 181mg; Carbs: 26.37g; Fibre: 1.6g; Sugar: 1.03g; Protein: 8.85g

Parmesan Garlic Bread

⏰ **Prep Time:** 10 minutes 🍱 **Cook:** 30 minutes ❖ **Serves:** 6 to 8

115g unsalted butter, melted
¼ teaspoon salt
75g grated Parmesan cheese
3 to 4 cloves garlic, minced
1 tablespoon chopped fresh parsley
455g frozen bread dough, defrosted
Olive oil
1 egg, beaten

1. Mix the melted butter, salt, Parmesan cheese, garlic and chopped parsley in a suitable bowl. 2. Roll the prepared dough out into a rectangle that measures 8 inches by 17 inches. 3. Spread the butter mixture over the prepared dough, leaving a half-inch border un-buttered along one of the long edges. Roll the prepared dough from one long edge to the other, ending with the un-buttered border. Pinch the seam shut tightly. Shape the log into a circle sealing the ends by pushing one end into the other and stretching the prepared dough around it. 4. Cut out a circle of aluminium foil that is the same size as the Ninja Foodi Pressure Steam Fryer basket. Brush the foil circle with oil and place an oven safe ramekin or glass in the centre. 5. Transfer the prepared dough ring to the aluminium foil circle, around the ramekin. This will help you make sure the prepared dough will fit in the basket and maintain its ring shape. Use kitchen shears to cut 8 slits around the outer edge of the prepared dough ring halfway to the centre. Brush the prepared dough ring with egg wash. 6. Brush the sides of the Cook & Crisp Basket with oil and transfer the prepared dough ring, foil circle and ramekin into the basket. 7. Slide the Cook & Crisp Basket back into the Pressure Steam Fryer, but do not turn it on. Let the prepared dough rise inside the Pressure Steam Fryer for around 30 minutes. 8. After the bread has proofed in the Ninja Foodi Pressure Steam Fryer for around 30 minutes. 9. Put on the Smart Lid on top of the Ninja Foodi Steam Fryer. 10. Move the Lid Slider to the "Air Fry/Stovetop". Select the "Air Fry" mode for cooking. 11. Cook the bread ring on the "Air Fry" mode at 170°C for 15 minutes. Flip the bread over by inverting it onto a plate or cutting board and sliding it back into the cook & crisp Basket. 12. Air-fry for another 15 minutes. Serve Warm.

Per serving: Calories: 334; Fat: 10.9g; Sodium: 354mg; Carbs: 20.5g; Fibre: 4.1g; Sugar 8.2g; Protein 06g

Chapter 1 Breakfast | 19

Blueberry Bread Pudding

⏰ Prep Time: 15 minutes 🍲 Cook: 15 minutes 🍽 Serves: 4

2 large eggs
240ml whole milk
2 tbsp. (30g) light brown sugar
1 tsp. pure vanilla extract
½ tsp. ground cinnamon
1 small loaf French bread, cut into ½" (1.3-cm) cubes (about 7 slices)
Nonstick cooking spray, for pan
75g blueberries, plus more for serving (optional)
240ml water
Pure maple syrup, for serving

1. Beat the eggs in a medium bowl, then the milk, brown sugar, vanilla and cinnamon, and whisk well until thoroughly combined. 2. Add the bread cubes and press into the liquid until completely submerged. Cover the bowl and refrigerate for 30 minutes (or overnight if you want to make it ahead). 3. Spray a cake pan with nonstick cooking spray. Take the bread mixture out of the refrigerator and gently fold in the blueberries. Pour the mixture into the prepared pan. 4. Pour the water into the pot and insert the rack. Cover the cake pan with foil and place on the rack. 5. Close the lid, turn the pressure release valve to SEAL position, and then move the slider to PRESSURE. Select HI and set the cooking time to 15 minutes. Press START/STOP to begin cooking. When finished, release the pressure quickly. 6. Cut the French toast and serve with maple syrup and more fresh blueberries, if desired.

Per Serving: Calories 296; Fat: 5.66g; Sodium: 372mg; Carbs: 52.06g; Fibre: 1.9g; Sugar: 24.43g; Protein: 9.41g

Bacon & Sweet Potatoes Stew

⏰ Prep Time: 15 minutes 🍲 Cook: 5 minutes 🍽 Serves: 4-6

1 tbsp. (15ml) extra-virgin olive oil
7 slices thick-cut bacon, diced
1 yellow onion, diced
1 tsp. Worcestershire sauce
60ml bourbon or beef stock
3 sweet potatoes (about 540g total), peeled and cut into large cubes
80ml water
Salt
Freshly ground black pepper
40g loosely packed light brown sugar
¼ tsp. cayenne pepper

1. Select SEAR/SAUTÉ. Select Lo3, and then press START/STOP to begin cooking. 2. When the pot is hot, add olive oil and bacon, and sauté them for 10 minutes until crispy; add the onion and sauté for 5 to 7 minutes until the onion is starting to caramalise. 3. Deglaze the pot with the Worcestershire and bourbon, and scrape up all the browned bacon bits from the bottom of the pot; sauté them for 2 more minutes. 4. Stop the process and stir in the sweet potatoes along with the water, plus salt and black pepper. 5. Close the lid, turn the pressure release valve to SEAL position, and then move the slider to PRESSURE. Select HI and set the cooking time to 3 minutes. Press START/STOP to begin cooking. When finished, release the pressure quickly. 6. Stir in the brown sugar and cayenne pepper. Let the potato mixture cool slightly before tasting and adjusting the salt and pepper, if needed. Enjoy.

Per Serving: Calories 291; Fat: 13.49g; Sodium: 253mg; Carbs: 35.43g; Fibre: 4.4g; Sugar: 2.76g; Protein: 7.99g

| Chapter 1 Breakfast

Blueberry Muffins

⏰ **Prep Time: 10 minutes** 🍳 **Cook: 14 minutes** 🍽 **Serves: 8**

155g flour
100g sugar
2 teaspoons baking powder
¼ teaspoon salt
80ml canola oil
1 egg
120ml milk
45g blueberries, fresh or frozen and thawed

1. In a suitable bowl, stir flour, sugar, baking powder, and salt. 2. In a separate bowl, mix cooking oil with egg, and milk and mix well. 3. Add egg mixture to dry recipe ingredients and stir just until moistened. 4. Gently stir in blueberries. 5. Spoon batter evenly into muffin cups. 6. Place the Cook & Crisp Basket in your Pressure Cooker Steam Fryer. 7. Place 4 muffin cups in "cook & crisp basket". 8. Put on the Smart Lid on top of the Ninja Foodi Steam Fryer. 9. Move the Lid Slider to the "Air Fry/Stovetop". Select the "Air Fry" mode for cooking. 10. Air fry at 165°C for around 12 to 14 minutes or until tops spring back when touched lightly. 11. Repeat previous step to cook remaining muffins.

Per serving: Calories: 219; Fat: 10g; Sodium: 891mg; Carbs: 22.9g; Fibre: 4g; Sugar 4g; Protein 13g

Sweet Bacon Knots

⏰ **Prep Time: 10 minutes** 🍳 **Cook: 8 minutes** 🍽 **Serves: 6**

455g maple smoked centre-cut bacon
60g maple syrup
45g brown sugar
Cracked black peppercorns

1. Place the Cook & Crisp Basket in your Pressure Cooker Steam Fryer. 2. Tie each bacon strip in a loose knot and place them on a suitable the Cook & Crisp Basket. 3. Mix the maple syrup and sugar in a suitable bowl. Brush each knot generously with this mixture and sprinkle with coarsely cracked black pepper. 4. Put on the Smart Lid on top of the Ninja Foodi Steam Fryer. 5. Move the Lid Slider to the "Air Fry/Stovetop". Select the "Air Fry" mode for cooking. 6. Air-fry the bacon knots in batches. Place one layer of knots in the Ninja Foodi Pressure Steam Fryer basket. Cook on the "Air Fry" mode at 200°C for around 5 minutes. Turn the bacon knots over. Cook on the "Air Fry" mode for 2 to 3 minutes. 7. Serve warm.

Per serving: Calories: 282; Fat: 19g; Sodium: 354mg; Carbs: 15g; Fibre: 5.1g; Sugar 8.2g; Protein 12g

Chapter 2 Vegetables and Sides

23	Garlic Brown Mushrooms	26	Indian Style Spaghetti Squash
23	Mashed Potatoes with Kale	27	Mashed Cauliflower Soup
24	Roasted Vegetable Bowls	27	Potato, Tomato and Cauliflower Curry
24	Spicy Potato Chunks	28	Air Fried Bell Peppers
25	Flavourful Sweet—Sour Red Cabbage	28	Collard Greens with Bacon
25	Tomato & Ricotta Cheese Risotto	29	Roasted Broccoli
26	Freekeh—Aubergine Bowls	29	Crispy Sweet Potatoes

Garlic Brown Mushrooms

⏰ Prep Time: 10 minutes   🍲 Cook: 9 minutes   🍽 Serves: 4

455g brown mushrooms, quartered
2 tablespoons sesame oil
1 tablespoon tamari sauce
1 garlic clove, pressed
Sea salt and black pepper, to taste

1. Place the Cook & Crisp Basket in your Pressure Cooker Steam Fryer. 2. Toss the mushrooms with the remaining ingredients. Toss until coated on all sides. 3. Arrange the mushrooms in the Ninja Foodi Pressure Steam Fryer basket. 4. Put on the Smart Lid on top of the Ninja Foodi Steam Fryer. 5. Move the Lid Slider to the "Air Fry/Stovetop". Select the "Air Fry" mode for cooking. 6. Cook your mushrooms at 200°C for about 7 minutes, shaking the basket halfway through the cooking time. 7. Serve in a plate and sprinkle with some sesame seeds if desired.

Per serving: Calories: 349; Fat: 2.9g; Sodium: 511mg; Carbs: 12g; Fibre: 3g; Sugar 8g; Protein 7g

Mashed Potatoes with Kale

⏰ Prep Time: 25 minutes   🍲 Cook: 10 minutes   🍽 Serves: 4-6

4 medium russet potatoes (910g), peeled and quartered
Salt
1 medium (230g) bunch lacinato kale, tough centre rib discarded, leaves chopped
4 tablespoons (½ stick) unsalted butter, at room temperature
4 green onions, thinly sliced
60ml to 120ml whole milk or heavy cream

1. Place the potatoes in the pot and add 240ml of water. Sprinkle them with ½ teaspoon salt. Put the kale on top of the potatoes, but don't stir it in. 2. Close the lid, turn the pressure release valve to SEAL position, and then move the slider to PRESSURE. Select HI and set the cooking time to 8 minutes. Press START/STOP to begin cooking. When finished, release the pressure quickly. 3. Set a colander in the sink and pour the potatoes and kale into the colander. Let the vegetables sit and cool for a few minutes; letting the steam evaporate will make the potatoes fluffier when you mash them. 4. While the vegetables cool, return the pot to the unit, add the butter, then select SEAR/SAUTÉ mode, and adjust to lo3. 5. When the butter has melted, add the green onions and cook them for 1 minute until tender; add the milk or cream and cook them for 1 minute to bring to a simmer. 6. Stop the process, and return the potatoes and kale to the pot and mash with a potato masher until the potatoes are mostly smooth. 7. Season the dish with salt and pepper. Enjoy.

Per Serving: Calories 270; Fat: 6.64g; Sodium: 54mg; Carbs: 45.39g; Fibre: 3.3g; Sugar: 2.31g; Protein: 8.88g

Roasted Vegetable Bowls

⏰ **Prep Time: 20 minutes** 🍲 **Cook: 60 minutes** 🍃 **Serves: 6**

455g sweet potatoes cut into 1-inch chunks
Extra-virgin olive oil, for drizzling
Fine sea salt and freshly ground black pepper
455g Brussels sprouts, cleaned and halved
1 bunch asparagus, cut into 1-inch pieces with woody stems removed (optional)
170g quinoa, rinsed
300ml water
6 tablespoons tahini
60ml freshly squeezed lemon juice
2 cloves garlic, minced
1 teaspoon ground cumin
125g chopped kale
150g cherry tomatoes, halved
1 cucumber, sliced

1. Arrange the sweet potatoes on a large baking pan and drizzle with olive oil. Toss the potatoes to coat with the oil, then season with salt and pepper. 2. Add the baking pan to the pot. Close the lid and move slider to AIR FRY/STOVETOP, then use the dial to select BAKE/ROAST. Adjust the cooking temperature to 200°C and set the cooking time to 25 minutes. Press START/STOP to begin cooking. 3. When cooked, transfer the sweet potatoes to a plate and clean the baking pan. 4. Place the Brussels sprouts and asparagus on the baking pan, then drizzle them with olive oil. Toss the sprouts and asparagus to coat with the oil, then season with salt and pepper; add the cooked sweet potatoes to them. 5. Cook them on BAKE/ROAST mode for 15 to 20 minutes until the vegetables are tender and golden. 6. Transfer the vegetables to a large plate and clean the pot. 7. Mix quinoa and 240ml of water in the pot. 8. Close the lid, turn the pressure release valve to SEAL position, and then move the slider to PRESSURE. Select HI and set the cooking time to 1 minute. Press START/STOP to begin cooking. When finished, release the pressure naturally. Fluff the quinoa. 9. Combine the tahini, lemon juice, garlic, cumin, remaining 60ml water, ¼ teaspoon salt, and several grinds of pepper in a small bowl. 10. To serve, fill each bowl with some chopped kale, cooked quinoa, roasted vegetables, cherry tomatoes, and cucumber. Drizzle the creamy tahini dressing over the top. 11. You can store the leftovers in four separate airtight containers—for the quinoa, the roasted vegetables, the raw vegetables, and the dressing—in the fridge for 5 days.

Per Serving: Calories 285; Fat: 10.66g; Sodium: 50mg; Carbs: 41.13g; Fibre: 11.4g; Sugar: 5.72g; Protein: 11.97g

Spicy Potato Chunks

⏰ **Prep Time: 10 minutes** 🍲 **Cook: 20 minutes** 🍃 **Serves: 4**

455g potatoes, diced into bite-sized chunks
1 tablespoon olive oil
Sea salt and black pepper, to taste
1 teaspoon chilli powder

1. Place the Cook & Crisp Basket in your Pressure Cooker Steam Fryer. 2. Toss the potatoes with the remaining recipe ingredients until well coated on all sides. 3. Arrange the potatoes in the Ninja Foodi Pressure Steam Fryer basket. 4. Put on the Smart Lid on top of the Ninja Foodi Steam Fryer. 5. Move the Lid Slider to the "Air Fry/Stovetop". Select the "Air Fry" mode for cooking. 6. Cook the potatoes at 200°C for about 13 minutes, shaking the basket halfway through the cooking time. 7. Serve.

Per serving: Calories: 289; Fat: 14g; Sodium: 791mg; Carbs: 18.9g; Fibre: 4.6g; Sugar 8g; Protein 6g

Flavourful Sweet-Sour Red Cabbage

Prep Time: 15 minutes Cook: 20 minutes Serves: 6

1 medium (910g) red cabbage
2 tablespoons olive oil
½ medium red onion, sliced
1½ teaspoons caraway seeds
½ teaspoon baking soda
3 tablespoons red wine vinegar
1 tablespoon brown sugar
Salt and freshly ground black pepper

1 Cut the cabbage into quarters. Remove and discard the tough white core from the base of each quarter. Shred the cabbage into ¼-inch-wide strips. Set aside. 2. Select SEAR/SAUTÉ. Select Hi5, and then press START/STOP to begin cooking. 3. When the pot is hot, heat the oil; add onion, caraway seeds, and baking soda to the pot, and cook them for 4 minutes until tender. 4. Add vinegar and brown sugar to the pot, and stop the process; stir in the cabbage, ½ teaspoon salt, and several grinds of black pepper. 5. Close the lid, turn the pressure release valve to SEAL position, and then move the slider to PRESSURE. Select HI and set the cooking time to 5 minutes. Press START/STOP to begin cooking. When finished, release the pressure quickly. 6. Season the dish with salt and pepper. Serve and enjoy.

Per Serving: Calories 93; Fat: 4.81g; Sodium: 144mg; Carbs: 12.24g; Fibre: 3.2g; Sugar: 6.7g; Protein: 2.16g

Tomato & Ricotta Cheese Risotto

Prep Time: 5 minutes Cook: 15 minutes Serves: 4

4 tablespoons unsalted butter
960ml chicken broth, divided
300g Arborio rice
2 tablespoons tomato paste
½ teaspoon salt
¼ teaspoon ground black pepper
60g ricotta cheese
5g julienned fresh basil leaves

1. Select SEAR/SAUTÉ. Select Hi5, and then press START/STOP to begin cooking. 2. When the pot is hot, heat the butter for 30 seconds until melted; add 240ml broth and rice, and cook them for 3 minutes until broth is absorbed by rice. 3. Add the remaining 720ml broth, tomato paste, salt, and pepper to the pot, and stop the process. 4. Close the lid, turn the pressure release valve to SEAL position, and then move the slider to PRESSURE. Select HI and set the cooking time to 10 minutes. Press START/STOP to begin cooking. When finished, release the pressure naturally. 5. Gently fold in ricotta cheese. 6. Ladle risotto into four bowls, garnish the dish with basil, and serve warm.

Per Serving: Calories 259; Fat: 19.52g; Sodium: 1240mg; Carbs: 25.34g; Fibre: 9.7g; Sugar: 2.63g; Protein: 10.11g

Freekeh-Aubergine Bowls

⏰ **Prep Time: 20 minutes** 🍲 **Cook: 10 minutes** 🍽 **Serves: 4**

1 medium aubergine, cut into 2-inch cubes
Salt
300ml store-bought vegetable or chicken broth, or homemade
40g cracked freekeh (such as Bob's Red Mill Cracked Freekeh)
1 tablespoon za'atar
2 tablespoons extra-virgin olive oil
1 (425g) can chickpeas, drained and rinsed
150g cherry tomatoes, halved
1 tablespoon red wine vinegar
1 medium garlic clove, finely chopped and smashed with the side of a knife
Freshly ground black pepper

1. Toss the aubergine with 1 teaspoon salt and set aside for 10 minutes to draw out the bitter juices. Pat the aubergine dry with paper towels. Rinse briefly and pat dry with paper towels again. 2. Combine the broth, freekeh, za'atar, ½ teaspoon salt, and 1 tablespoon of the oil in the pot; add the chickpeas and then layer the aubergine on top, but don't stir it into the broth mixture. 3. Close the lid, turn the pressure release valve to SEAL position, and then move the slider to PRESSURE. Select HI and set the cooking time to 5 minutes. Press START/STOP to begin cooking. When finished, release the pressure naturally. 4. Transfer the grain mixture to a large serving bowl. 5. In a small bowl, whisk together the remaining 1 tablespoon oil with the tomatoes, vinegar, garlic, and several grinds of pepper. 6. Gently toss the dressing with the grain mixture and serve warm or at room temperature.

Per Serving: Calories 197; Fat: 5.09g; Sodium: 530mg; Carbs: 33.77g; Fibre: 9.1g; Sugar: 16.74g; Protein: 7.06g

Indian Style Spaghetti Squash

⏰ **Prep Time: 30 minutes** 🍲 **Cook: 10 minutes** 🍽 **Serves: 4**

1 medium (1135g) spaghetti squash, halved lengthwise and seeded
3 tablespoons unsalted butter or ghee
1½ teaspoons brown mustard seeds
1 teaspoon cumin seeds
3 medium garlic cloves, chopped
1 medium tomato, chopped
Salt and freshly ground black pepper

1. Place a rack in the bottom of the pot and add 360ml cold water. Place the squash halves cut-side up on the rack. 2. Close the lid, turn the pressure release valve to SEAL position, and then move the slider to PRESSURE. Select HI and set the cooking time to 8 minutes. Press START/STOP to begin cooking. When finished, release the pressure quickly. 3. Transfer the squash to a cutting board. Drag a fork crosswise over the squash to scrape out the flesh into strands; discard the skins. Place the squash in a large serving bowl and cover with foil. 4. Discard the steaming water, dry out the pot, and return it to the appliance. 5. Select SEAR/SAUTÉ. Select Lo3, and then press START/STOP to begin cooking. 6. When the pot is heated, melt the butter, then add the mustard seeds and cumin seeds, cooking for 1 minute until the seeds start to pop; add garlic and tomato, and cook them for 1 minute until fragrant. 7. Stop the process, and pour the butter mixture over the squash; season them with salt and pepper, and toss them to combine well. 8. Serve and enjoy.

Per Serving: Calories 75; Fat: 6.34g; Sodium: 8mg; Carbs: 4.04g; Fibre: 1.1g; Sugar: 1.97g; Protein: 1.64g

| Chapter 2 Vegetables and Sides

Mashed Cauliflower Soup

⏰ **Prep Time: 15 minutes**　🍲 **Cook: 20 minutes**　🍃 **Serves: 6**

1 large head cauliflower, chopped (660g)
120ml chicken broth
2 garlic cloves, crushed
1 tsp. whole peppercorns
1 bay leaf

½ tsp. salt

1. Place cauliflower in the pot, and add water to cover. Bring to a boil at Hi5 on SEAR/SAUTÉ mode and then reduce the cooking temperature to Lo2; cover the saucepan and simmer them for 10 to 12 minutes until tender. Drain the cauliflower and then return to pot. 2. Combine the rest of the ingredients in a small saucepan, and bring to a boil. 3. Immediately remove the saucepan from heat and strain, discarding garlic, peppercorns and bay leaf. 4. Add broth to cauliflower. Mash them until reaching desired consistency. Serve and enjoy.

Per Serving: Calories 45; Fat: 1.54g; Sodium: 290mg; Carbs: 2.72g; Fibre: 0.9g; Sugar: 0.9g; Protein: 5.26g

Potato, Tomato and Cauliflower Curry

⏰ **Prep Time: 20 minutes**　🍲 **Cook: 10 minutes**　🍃 **Serves: 4**

2 tablespoons safflower oil
1 tablespoon brown mustard seeds
1 medium yellow onion, chopped
1 tablespoon hot curry powder
375g chopped ripe tomatoes
3 medium Yukon Gold potatoes (about 230g), unpeeled, cut into 1-inch cubes
Salt and freshly ground black pepper
1 medium (680g) cauliflower, cut into large (3-inch) florets, stalk and core discarded

1. Select SEAR/SAUTÉ. Select Lo3, and then press START/STOP to begin cooking. 2. When the pot is hot, heat the oil, then add the mustard seeds and cook them for 1 minute until they have popped and turned gray; add onion and curry powder, and cook them for 4 minutes until the onion is tender; add tomatoes and cook for 2 minutes until they break down a bit. 3. Stop the process, and stir in the potatoes, 120ml water, 1 teaspoon salt, and several grinds of pepper; place the cauliflower florets on top of the potato mixture without stirring. 4. Close the lid, turn the pressure release valve to SEAL position, and then move the slider to PRESSURE. Select LO and set the cooking time to 2 minutes. Press START/STOP to begin cooking. When finished, release the pressure quickly. 5. Transfer the mixture to a large serving bowl and gently break up the cauliflower with a spoon. Serve immediately.

Per Serving: Calories 344; Fat: 8.39g; Sodium: 66mg; Carbs: 61.73g; Fibre: 11.2g; Sugar: 7.75g; Protein: 9.85g

Air Fried Bell Peppers

⏱ **Prep Time: 10 minutes** 🍲 **Cook: 15 minutes** ◆ **Serves: 3**

455g bell peppers, seeded and halved
1 chilli pepper, seeded
2 tablespoons olive oil
Salt and black pepper, to taste
1 teaspoon granulated garlic

1. Place the Cook & Crisp Basket in your Pressure Cooker Steam Fryer. 2. Toss the peppers with the remaining ingredients; place them in the cook and crisp basket. 3. Put on the Smart Lid on top of the Ninja Foodi Steam Fryer. 4. Move the Lid Slider to the "Air Fry/Stovetop". Select the "Air Fry" mode for cooking. 5. Cook the peppers at 200°C for about 15 minutes, shaking the basket halfway through the cooking time. 6. Taste, adjust the seasonings and serve at room temperature. Serve.

Per serving: Calories: 270; Fat: 10.9g; Sodium: 454mg; Carbs: 10g; Fibre: 3.1g; Sugar 5.2g; Protein 10g

Collard Greens with Bacon

⏱ **Prep Time: 15 minutes** 🍲 **Cook: 15 minutes** ◆ **Serves: 4**

3 slices thick-cut pepper bacon, chopped
1 small yellow onion, chopped
3 medium garlic cloves, chopped
180ml store-bought chicken or vegetable broth, or homemade
2 large (260g) bunches collard greens, tough centre stems discarded, leaves torn
2 tablespoons cider vinegar or red wine vinegar
1 teaspoon smoked paprika
Salt and freshly ground black pepper

1. Select SEAR/SAUTÉ. Select Lo3, and then press START/STOP to begin cooking. 2. When the pot is hot, add bacon and onion, and cook them for 8 minutes until the bacon is browned; add garlic and sauté them for 45 seconds until fragrant. 3. Stop the process, add broth and scrape up the browned bits on the bottom of the pot, then add greens, vinegar, paprika, ½ teaspoon salt, and several grinds of pepper and toss them to coat the greens with the liquid. 4. Close the lid, turn the pressure release valve to SEAL position, and then move the slider to PRESSURE. Select HI and set the cooking time to 5 minutes. Press START/STOP to begin cooking. When finished, release the pressure naturally. 5. Season the dish with salt and pepper. Serve the greens immediately.

Per Serving: Calories 88; Fat: 2.81g; Sodium: 220mg; Carbs: 13.89g; Fibre: 3.5g; Sugar: 4.28g; Protein: 4.36g

Chapter 2 Vegetables and Sides

Roasted Broccoli

⏰ **Prep Time: 10 minutes**　🍲 **Cook: 8 minutes**　🍽 **Serves: 3**

315g broccoli florets
1 ½ tablespoons olive oil
1 teaspoon garlic powder
½ teaspoon onion powder
½ teaspoon mustard seeds
Sea salt and black pepper, to taste
2 tablespoons pepitas, roasted

1. Place the Cook & Crisp Basket in your Pressure Cooker Steam Fryer. 2. Toss the broccoli florets with the olive oil, garlic powder, onion powder, mustard seeds, salt, and black pepper. 3. Put on the Smart Lid on top of the Ninja Foodi Steam Fryer. 4. Move the Lid Slider to the "Air Fry/Stovetop". Select the "Air Fry" mode for cooking. 5. Cook the broccoli florets at 200°C for around 6 minutes, shaking the basket halfway through the cooking time. 6. Top with roasted pepitas and serve warm. Serve.

Per serving: Calories: 334; Fat: 7.9g; Sodium: 704mg; Carbs: 6g; Fibre: 3.6g; Sugar 6g; Protein 18g

Crispy Sweet Potatoes

⏰ **Prep Time: 10 minutes**　🍲 **Cook: 40 minutes**　🍽 **Serves: 4**

455g sweet potatoes, scrubbed and halved
3 tablespoons olive oil
1 teaspoon paprika
Sea salt and black pepper, to taste

1. Place the Cook & Crisp Basket in your Pressure Cooker Steam Fryer. 2. Toss the halved sweet potatoes with the olive oil, paprika, salt, and black pepper. 3. Put on the Smart Lid on top of the Ninja Foodi Steam Fryer. 4. Move the Lid Slider to the "Air Fry/Stovetop". Select the "Air Fry" mode for cooking. 5. Cook the sweet potatoes at 195°C for around 35 minutes, shaking the basket halfway through the cooking time. 6. Taste and adjust the seasonings. Serve.

Per serving: Calories: 372; Fat: 20g; Sodium: 891mg; Carbs: 29g; Fibre: 3g; Sugar 8g; Protein 7g

Chapter 3 Snacks and Appetisers

31 Loaded Baby Potatoes
31 Barbecue Beef Meatballs
32 Chicken Wings with Barbecue Sauce
32 Classic Deviled Eggs
33 Pepperoni Pizza Bombs with Marinara Sauce
33 Olive-Stuffed Jalapeños
34 Cheese Chicken Meatballs
34 Cheese Cauliflower Pizza Crusts
35 Savoury Buffalo Chicken Wings
35 Party Chex Nuts Snack
36 Parmesan Breaded Aubergine Slices
36 Easy Air-Fried Pumpkin Seeds

Loaded Baby Potatoes

⏱ **Prep Time: 15 minutes** 🍲 **Cook: 20 minutes** ❖ **Serves: 10**

4 slices bacon, halved
910g baby yellow potatoes (approximately 10), scrubbed
240ml water
2 tablespoons unsalted butter
60g sour cream
30g grated Cheddar cheese
2 tablespoons whole milk
½ teaspoon salt
½ teaspoon ground black pepper
2 tablespoons chopped fresh chives

1. Use a fork to pierce each potato four times. Set aside. 2. Select SEAR/SAUTÉ. Select Hi5, and then press START/STOP to begin cooking. 3. When the pot is hot, cook the bacon for 4 minutes until crisp; transfer the bacon to a plate and set aside, leaving rendered fat in the pot; add potatoes to the pot and sauté them for 3 minutes to absorb some of the bacon flavour. 4. Stop the process and pour the water in the pot. 5. Close the lid, turn the pressure release valve to SEAL position, and then move the slider to PRESSURE. Select HI and set the cooking time to 7 minutes. Press START/STOP to begin cooking. When finished, release the pressure quickly. 8. Transfer the potatoes to a plate. Let them cool for 5 minutes until you can handle them. 9. Cut potatoes in half lengthwise. Scoop out approximately half of the potato, creating a boat. Add scooped-out potato to a medium bowl. Place potato halves on a baking sheet lined with parchment paper. 10. In medium bowl with scooped-out potatoes, add butter, sour cream, Cheddar cheese, milk, salt, and pepper. Combine them until ingredients are well distributed. Spoon the mixture into potato halves. 11. Place the potato halves to the cleaned pot. Close the lid and move slider to AIR FRY/STOVETOP, then use the dial to select BAKE/ROAST. Adjust the cooking temperature to 175°C and set the cooking time to 5 minutes. Press START/STOP to begin cooking. 12. Crumble the bacon. 13. Transfer the potato halves to a serving dish; garnish the dish with bacon and chives. 14. Serve and enjoy.

Per Serving: Calories 226; Fat: 12.66g; Sodium: 484mg; Carbs: 23.47g; Fibre: 2g; Sugar: 0.57g; Protein: 4.7g

Barbecue Beef Meatballs

⏱ **Prep Time: 10 minutes** 🍲 **Cook: 10 minutes** ❖ **Serves: 6**

455g ground beef
1 large egg
45g bread crumbs
1 teaspoon minced onion
¼ teaspoon garlic powder
¼ teaspoon salt
⅛ teaspoon black pepper
2 tablespoons olive oil
240ml water
285g barbecue sauce
170g honey
2 tablespoons brown sugar

1. Combine ground beef, egg, bread crumbs, onion, garlic powder, salt, and pepper in a medium bowl for 3 minutes or until fully combined. 2. Roll beef mixture into golf ball–sized meatballs. 3. Select SEAR/SAUTÉ. Select Hi5, and then press START/STOP to begin cooking. 4. When the pot is hot, heat the oil; brown the meatballs for 1 minute on each side until golden brown on the outside. Transfer the meatballs to a bowl and set aside. Stop the process. 5. Pour water into the pot and deglaze the pot. 6. Whisk together barbecue sauce, honey, and brown sugar in a small bowl. Place the meatballs in the pot and pour the sauce over them, turn the meatballs to coat them well. 7. Close the lid, turn the pressure release valve to SEAL position, and then move the slider to PRESSURE. Select HI and set the cooking time to 4 minutes. Press START/STOP to begin cooking. When finished, release the pressure naturally. 8. Serve the meatballs on toothpicks.

Per Serving: Calories 415; Fat: 14.09g; Sodium: 655mg; Carbs: 51.22g; Fibre: 1.1g; Sugar: 44.61g; Protein: 21.78g

Chapter 3 Snacks and Appetisers

Chicken Wings with Barbecue Sauce

⏱ **Prep Time: 10 minutes** 🍲 **Cook: 15 minutes** ❖ **Serves: 4**

910g frozen chicken wings
½ tablespoon garlic salt
360ml water
285g barbecue sauce

1. Toss the chicken wings in garlic salt in a large bowl so they are evenly coated. 2. Pour water into the pot and place in the rack. 3. Place wings in a spring-form pan. Create a foil sling and lower pan on the rack. 4. Close the lid, turn the pressure release valve to SEAL position, and then move the slider to PRESSURE. Select HI and set the cooking time to 15 minutes. Press START/STOP to begin cooking. When finished, release the pressure naturally. 5. Remove the wings and brush with barbecue sauce. Serve hot.

Per Serving: Calories 410; Fat: 8.48g; Sodium: 920mg; Carbs: 29.51g; Fibre: 0.7g; Sugar: 23.78g; Protein: 50.48g

Classic Deviled Eggs

⏱ **Prep Time: 15 minutes** 🍲 **Cook: 5 minutes** ❖ **Serves: 4**

360ml water
6 large eggs
30g mayonnaise
30g mustard
1 teaspoon white vinegar
⅛ teaspoon salt
⅛ teaspoon black pepper
¼ teaspoon paprika

1. Pour water into the pot. Place a rack in the pot and arrange eggs on top of rack. 2. Close the lid, turn the pressure release valve to SEAL position, and then move the slider to PRESSURE. Select HI and set the cooking time to 5 minutes. Press START/STOP to begin cooking. When finished, release the pressure naturally. 3. Carefully place eggs into a bowl of ice water. Leave eggs in ice bath 5 minutes. Remove eggs and peel. 4. Slice eggs in half and carefully scoop out yolk with a spoon. Place all yolks in a small bowl. 5. Add mayonnaise, mustard, vinegar, salt, and pepper to bowl of yolks. Mix them until fully combined. 6. Scoop heaping spoonfuls of egg yolk mixture into centre of halved hard-boiled eggs. 7. Sprinkle paprika on top of each deviled egg. 8. Chill eggs up to 24 hours until ready to be served.

Per Serving: Calories 151; Fat: 10.76g; Sodium: 348mg; Carbs: 1.47g; Fibre: 0.5g; Sugar: 0.47g; Protein: 11.35g

| Chapter 3 Snacks and Appetisers

Pepperoni Pizza Bombs with Marinara Sauce

⏲ Prep Time: 10 minutes　🍲 Cook: 12 minutes　🍽 Serves: 9 pizza bites

40g gluten-free all-purpose flour
¼ teaspoon salt
¼ teaspoon baking powder
70g small-diced pepperoni
55g cream cheese, room temperature
30g shredded mozzarella cheese
½ teaspoon Italian seasoning
2 tablespoons whole milk
1 teaspoon olive oil
125g marinara sauce, warmed

1. Place the Cook & Crisp Basket in your Pressure Cooker Steam Fryer. 2. In a suitable bowl, mix flour, salt, and baking powder. 3. In a suitable bowl, mix remaining ingredients, except marinara sauce. Add dry recipe ingredients to bowl and mix until well mixed. 4. Form mixture into nine (1") balls and place on the Cook & Crisp Basket. Put on the Smart Lid on top of the Ninja Foodi Steam Fryer. 5. Move the Lid Slider to the "Air Fry/Stovetop". Select the "Air Fry" mode for cooking. Adjust the cooking temperature to 160°C. 6. Cook for 12 minutes. 7. Transfer balls to a suitable plate. Serve warm with marinara sauce.

Per serving: Calories 217; Fat: 5.1g; Sodium 624mg; Carbs: 6.8g; Fibre: 0.8g; Sugars 1.8g; Protein 31.1g

Olive-Stuffed Jalapeños

⏲ Prep Time: 10 minutes　🍲 Cook: 8 minutes　🍽 Serves: 5

60g plain cream cheese
30g finely grated Cheddar cheese
2 tablespoons chopped black olives
5 medium jalapeño peppers, cut lengthwise, seeded

1. Place the Cook & Crisp Basket in your Pressure Cooker Steam Fryer. 2. In a suitable bowl, cream cheese, Cheddar cheese, and black olives. 3. Press cream cheese mixture into each jalapeño half. 4. Lay stuffed peppers in ungreased "cook & crisp basket". 5. Put on the Smart Lid on top of the Ninja Foodi Steam Fryer. 6. Move the Lid Slider to the "Air Fry/Stovetop". Select the "Air Fry" mode for cooking. 7. Adjust the cooking temperature to 175°C for 8 minutes. 8. Once done, transfer stuffed peppers to a suitable serving plate and serve warm.

Per serving: Calories 319; Fat: 15.6g; Sodium 99mg; Carbs: 4.8g; Fibre: 0.7g; Sugars 2.9g; Protein 38.5g

Cheese Chicken Meatballs

⏰ **Prep Time:** 10 minutes 🍲 **Cook:** 20 minutes ❖ **Serves:** 6

455g ground chicken
1 large egg
45g bread crumbs
110g shredded carrots
15g minced green onions
30g minced celery
2 cloves garlic, minced
2 ounces blue cheese crumbles
2 tablespoons olive oil
120ml water
235g buffalo sauce

1. Combine the chicken, egg, bread crumbs, carrots, green onions, celery, garlic, and blue cheese in a medium bowl for 3 minutes until fully combined, about 3 minutes. 2. Roll chicken mixture into golf ball–sized meatballs. 3. Select SEAR/SAUTÉ. Select Hi5, and then press START/STOP to begin cooking. 4. When the pot is hot, heat the oil, and brown the meatballs for 1 minute on each side until golden brown on the outside. Transfer the meatballs to a bowl and set aside. 5. Pour water into the pot and deglaze the pot. Stop the process. 6. Place meatballs in the pot and pour buffalo sauce on top. Turn meatballs to coat in sauce. 7. Close the lid, turn the pressure release valve to SEAL position, and then move the slider to PRESSURE. Select HI and set the cooking time to 15 minutes. Press START/STOP to begin cooking. When finished, release the pressure naturally. 8. Serve the meatballs on toothpicks with drizzled sauce from pot.

Per Serving: Calories 278; Fat: 19.63g; Sodium: 510mg; Carbs: 6.93g; Fibre: 1.5g; Sugar: 2.95g; Protein: 18.33g

Cheese Cauliflower Pizza Crusts

⏰ **Prep Time:** 10 minutes 🍲 **Cook:** 30 minutes ❖ **Serves:** 2

115g cauliflower rice
1 large egg
60g grated mozzarella cheese
1 tablespoon grated Parmesan cheese
1 clove garlic, peeled and minced
1 teaspoon Italian seasoning
⅛ teaspoon salt
Cooking oil

1. Place the deluxe reversible rack in your Pressure Cooker Steam Fryer. 2. In a suitable bowl, mix all the recipe ingredients. 3. Divide mixture in half and spread into two pizza suitable pans greased with preferred cooking oil. 4. Place one pan in the deluxe reversible rack. Put on the Smart Lid on top of the Ninja Foodi Steam Fryer. Move the Lid Slider to the "Air Fry/Stovetop". Select the "Air Fry" mode for cooking. 5. Adjust the cooking temperature to 200°C. 6. Cook for 12 minutes. Once done, remove pan and repeat with second pan. 7. Top crusts with your favourite toppings. Cook for an additional 3 minutes.

Per serving: Calories 309; Fat: 17.4g; Sodium 348mg; Carbs: 4.8g; Fibre: 1.9g; Sugars 0.6g; Protein 33.4g

Chapter 3 Snacks and Appetisers

Savoury Buffalo Chicken Wings

⏱ **Prep Time: 10 minutes** 🍲 **Cook: 15 minutes** ❖ **Serves: 4**

910g frozen chicken wings
½ tablespoon Cajun seasoning
360ml water
235g buffalo wing sauce

1. Toss the chicken wings with Cajun seasoning in a large bowl so they are evenly coated. 2. Pour water in the pot and place in the rack. 3. Place wings in a spring-form pan. Create a foil sling and lower pan into the pot. 4. Close the lid, turn the pressure release valve to SEAL position, and then move the slider to PRESSURE. Select HI and set the cooking time to 15 minutes. Press START/STOP to begin cooking. When finished, release the pressure naturally. 5. Remove the wings and brush with buffalo sauce. Serve hot.

Per Serving: Calories 311; Fat: 9.63g; Sodium: 311mg; Carbs: 1.29g; Fibre: 0.2g; Sugar: 0.13g; Protein: 51.1g

Party Chex Nuts Snack

⏱ **Prep Time: 5 minutes** 🍲 **Cook: 5 minutes** ❖ **Serves: 4**

60g Rice Chex
60g Corn Chex
30g mixed nuts
¼ teaspoon salt
3 tablespoons butter, melted

1. Place the Cook & Crisp Basket in your Pressure Cooker Steam Fryer. 2. In a suitable bowl, mix all the recipe ingredients. 3. Place Chex mixture into ungreased "cook & crisp basket". 4. Put on the Smart Lid on top of the Ninja Foodi Steam Fryer. 5. Move the Lid Slider to the "Air Fry/Stovetop". Select the "Air Fry" mode for cooking. Adjust the cooking temperature to 175°C. Cook for 3 minutes. 6. Shake basket, then cook an additional 2 minutes. 7. Transfer mixture to a serving bowl. Let cool 5 minutes, then serve warm.

Per serving: Calories 307; Fat: 15.5g; Sodium 720mg; Carbs: 6.6g; Fibre: 1g; Sugars 2.8g; Protein 36.6g

Chapter 3 Snacks and Appetisers

Parmesan Breaded Aubergine Slices

⏰ Prep Time: 10 minutes   🍲 Cook: 12 minutes   ❖ Serves: 2

2 large eggs
2 tablespoons whole milk
120g gluten-free bread crumbs
50g grated Parmesan cheese
1 teaspoon salt
1 medium aubergine, cut into ½" rounds, then sliced
125g marinara sauce, warmed

1. Place the Cook & Crisp Basket in your Pressure Cooker Steam Fryer. 2. Mix eggs and milk in a suitable bowl. In a separate shallow dish, mix bread crumbs, Parmesan cheese, and salt. 3. Dip aubergine in egg mixture. Dredge in bread crumb mixture. 4. Place aubergine fries in ungreased "cook & crisp basket". Put on the Smart Lid on top of the Ninja Foodi Steam Fryer. Move the Lid Slider to the "Air Fry/Stovetop". Select the "Air Fry" mode for cooking. 5. Adjust the cooking temperature to 200°C. 6. Cook for 5 minutes. Flip fries, then cook an additional 5 minutes. Flip once more. Cook for an additional 2 minutes. 7. Transfer fries to a suitable plate and serve with warmed marinara sauce on the side for dipping.

Per serving: Calories 314; Fat: 8.7g; Sodium 337mg; Carbs: 21.2g; Fibre: 4.1g; Sugars 16g; Protein 37.9g

Easy Air-Fried Pumpkin Seeds

⏰ Prep Time: 10 minutes   🍲 Cook: 13 minutes   ❖ Serves: 4

200g fresh pumpkin seeds, rinsed and dried
2 teaspoons olive oil
½ teaspoon salt

1. Place the Cook & Crisp Basket in your Pressure Cooker Steam Fryer. 2. In a suitable bowl, toss seeds with oil and ½ teaspoon salt. 3. Place seeds in ungreased "cook & crisp basket". 4. Put on the Smart Lid on top of the Ninja Foodi Steam Fryer. 5. Move the Lid Slider to the "Air Fry/Stovetop". Select the "Air Fry" mode for cooking. 6. Adjust the cooking temperature to 160°C. 7. Cook for 7 minutes. Using a spatula, turn seeds, then cook an additional 6 minutes. 8. Transfer seeds to a suitable bowl and let cool 5 minutes before serving.

Per serving: Calories 481; Fat: 14.6g; Sodium 285mg; Carbs: 57.5g; Fibre: 7.3g; Sugars 1g; Protein 31.1g

Chapter 3 Snacks and Appetisers

Chapter 4 Poultry Mains

38	Crisp Chicken Tenders	41	Pasta Chicken Puttanesca
38	Chicken & Ziti Casserole	42	Korean Chicken Wings
39	Cider & Mustard—Braised Chicken Thighs	42	Chicken Fajita Rollups
39	Turkey Bolognese with Spaghetti Squash	43	Turkey Breast with Mustard—Maple Glaze
40	Chicken Thighs & Quinoa Bowls	43	Crispy Oats Crusted Chicken Drumsticks
40	Chicken Bacon Salad	44	Delicious Chicken Mushroom Kabobs
41	Pulled Turkey	44	Juicy Chicken Thighs

Crisp Chicken Tenders

⏲ Prep Time: 10 minutes 🍲 Cook: 15 minutes 🍽 Serves: 4-6

40g coconut flour
1 tablespoon spicy brown mustard
2 beaten eggs
455g of chicken tenders

1. Place the Cook & Crisp Basket in your Pressure Cooker Steam Fryer. 2. Season tenders with pepper and salt. 3. Place a thin layer of mustard onto tenders and then dredge in flour and dip in egg. Coat in the flour again. 4. Place tenders in the Cook & Crisp Basket. Put on the Smart Lid on top of the Ninja Foodi Steam Fryer. Move the Lid Slider to the "Air Fry/Stovetop". Select the "Air Fry" mode for cooking. Cook for 10 to 15 minutes at 200°C till crispy.

Per serving: Calories: 478; Fat: 12.9g; Sodium: 414mg; Carbs: 11g; Fibre: 5g; Sugar 9g; Protein 11g

Chicken & Ziti Casserole

⏲ Prep Time: 5 minutes 🍲 Cook: 10 minutes 🍽 Serves: 4

30g sliced almonds
1 tablespoon butter
1 small yellow onion, chopped (65g)
455g unseasoned chicken breast cut for stir-fry, any flavouring packets discarded; or 455g boneless skinless chicken breast, cut into ½ x ½-inch strips
1¼ teaspoons dried sage
1 teaspoon dried thyme
½ teaspoon dried oregano
¼ teaspoon grated nutmeg
¼ teaspoon table salt
600ml chicken broth
230g dried ziti
160ml regular or low-fat evaporated milk
120g packed sun-dried tomatoes, sliced into very thin strips
120g heavy cream
1½ tablespoons all-purpose flour
30g finely grated Parmigiano-Reggiano

1. Cook the sliced almonds in a medium dry skillet over medium-low heat for 2 minutes until lightly toasted. Pour the almonds into a small bowl and set aside. 2. Select SEAR/SAUTÉ. Select Lo3, and then press START/STOP to begin cooking. 3. When the pot is hot, melt the butter; add onion and cook for 3 minutes until softened; add chicken, sage, thyme, oregano, nutmeg, and salt, and cook them for 2 minutes juts until the chicken loses its raw color. 4. Stop the process, and stir in the broth, ziti, evaporated milk, and sun-dried tomatoes until uniform. 5. Close the lid, turn the pressure release valve to SEAL position, and then move the slider to PRESSURE. Select HI and set the cooking time to 7 minutes. Press START/STOP to begin cooking. When finished, release the pressure naturally. 6. Whisk the cream and flour in a small bowl until the flour dissolves. 7. Keep stirring the sauce in the pot at Lo2 on SEAR/SAUTÉ mode until comes to a simmer. Whisk the cream mixture one time to make sure the flour is thoroughly combined. Stir this slurry into the pot and continue cooking for 2 minutes until thickened, stirring almost constantly. 8. Stir in the cheese and set the lid askew over the insert for a couple of minutes to blend the flavours. 9. Sprinkle the toasted almonds over individual servings.

Per Serving: Calories 346; Fat: 13.01g; Sodium: 1077mg; Carbs: 54.38g; Fibre: 8.4g; Sugar: 37.9g; Protein: 10.58g

| Chapter 4 Poultry Mains

Cider & Mustard-Braised Chicken Thighs

⏰ **Prep Time: 10 minutes** 🍲 **Cook: 35 minutes** 🍽 **Serves: 4**

2 slices thick-cut bacon, chopped
8 bone-in chicken thighs, skin removed and fat trimmed
Salt and freshly ground black pepper
230g quartered cremini mushrooms
2 large shallots, thinly sliced (120g)
360ml bottled hard apple cider
2 tablespoons grainy mustard

1. Season the chicken all over with salt and pepper. 2. Select SEAR/SAUTÉ. Select Lo3, and then press START/STOP to begin cooking. 3. When the pot is hot, cook the bacon for 3 to 4 minutes until browned. Transfer the bacon to a bowl with a slotted spoon; leave the drippings in the pot. 4. Add the chicken thighs to the pot and cook for 3 minutes until browned on one side. Transfer them to a plate. 5. Add the mushrooms and shallots to the pot and sauté them for 3 minutes until the shallots are tender; add the cider and mustard, then bring the mixture to a simmer while scraping up any browned bits from the bottom of the pot. 6. Stop the process, and add all the chicken, any accumulated juices, and the bacon to the pot. 7. Close the lid, turn the pressure release valve to SEAL position, and then move the slider to PRESSURE. Select HI and set the cooking time to 20 minutes. Press START/STOP to begin cooking. When finished, release the pressure quickly. 8. Using a slotted spoon, transfer the chicken and vegetables to a serving dish. Cover the dish with foil and set it aside. 9. Bring the liquid in the pot to a simmer at Lo2 at SEAR/SAUTÉ mode; skim off any liquid fat that collects on the surface of the sauce and discard it; cook the sauce for 5 minutes until the sauce is reduced by half. 10. Stop the process, and pour the sauce over the chicken thighs. 11. Serve warm.

Per Serving: Calories 975; Fat: 69.92g; Sodium: 468mg; Carbs: 15.12g; Fibre: 1.6g; Sugar: 10.66g; Protein: 68.87g

Turkey Bolognese with Spaghetti Squash

⏰ **Prep Time: 5 minutes** 🍲 **Cook: 25 minutes** 🍽 **Serves: 4**

1 tablespoon extra-virgin olive oil
1 yellow onion, chopped
2 cloves garlic, minced
455g ground turkey
Fine sea salt
1 (800g) can diced tomatoes
2 celery stalks, diced
2 carrots, diced
1 tablespoon aged balsamic vinegar
1 teaspoon pure maple syrup
½ teaspoon dried oregano
1 teaspoon dried basil
1 (1365g) spaghetti squash
60ml full-fat coconut milk (optional)
Freshly ground black pepper
Fresh basil, for garnish (optional)

1. Pour the diced tomatoes with their juices into a blender and blend them until smooth. Set aside. 2. Wash the spaghetti squash and carefully pierce the skin once with a sharp knife to vent. 3. Select SEAR/SAUTÉ. Select Lo2, and then press START/STOP to begin cooking. 4. When the pot is hot, add olive oil, onion, garlic, turkey, and 1 teaspoon salt to the pot, and sauté them for 8 minutes until the turkey is browned. 5. Stop the process, and add blended tomatoes, the celery, carrots, vinegar, maple syrup, oregano, basil, and ½ teaspoon salt to the pot; stir them well. Place the whole squash directly into the sauce, pierced side up. 6. Close the lid, turn the pressure release valve to SEAL position, and then move the slider to PRESSURE. Select HI and set the cooking time to 15 minutes. Press START/STOP to begin cooking. When finished, release the pressure naturally. 7. Lift the spaghetti squash out of the pot. Transfer it to a cutting board to cool slightly. Stir the coconut milk into the sauce and season with salt and pepper, to taste. 8. Slice the cooked squash in half crosswise and use a spoon to scoop out the seeds from the centre. Then, use a fork to scrape out the "noodles" from the squash and place them on plates. 9. Spoon the Bolognese sauce on top of the noodles and serve. 10. You can store the leftovers in an airtight container in the fridge for 3 or 4 days.

Per Serving: Calories 725; Fat: 58.57g; Sodium: 398mg; Carbs: 26.68g; Fibre: 7.4g; Sugar: 9.99g; Protein: 25.17g

Chicken Thighs & Quinoa Bowls

⏰ Prep Time: 25 minutes   🍲 Cook: 15 minutes   ❖ Serves: 4

2 teaspoons taco seasoning
6 to 8 chicken thighs, fat trimmed
2 tablespoons olive oil
195g fresh refrigerated tomato salsa
240ml plus 1 tablespoon store-bought chicken broth, or homemade
135g red quinoa, rinsed
1 (425g) can black beans, drained and rinsed, or 270g home-cooked beans
Salt and freshly ground black pepper
235g prepared guacamole
Optional Toppings:
Shredded cheddar cheese
Sour cream
Sliced olives

1. Rub the taco seasoning into the chicken thighs. 2. Select SEAR/SAUTÉ. Select Lo3, and then press START/STOP to begin cooking. 3. When the pot is hot, heat the oil, and brown the chicken thighs for 3 minutes on one side only until golden brown. You can cook them in batches. 4. Stop the process, and drain off the fat in the pot and return the pot to the unit. 5. Add 130g of the salsa and 60ml of the broth to the pot and scrape up the browned bits on the bottom of the pot. Add the chicken and any accumulated juices to the pot. Spoon the remaining 65g salsa over the chicken. 6. Place the rack in the pot over the chicken. 7. Combine the quinoa and remaining 180ml plus 1 tablespoon broth in a baking pan; spoon the beans over the quinoa mixture, but don't stir them in. Place the pan on the rack. 8. Close the lid, turn the pressure release valve to SEAL position, and then move the slider to PRESSURE. Select HI and set the cooking time to 12 minutes. Press START/STOP to begin cooking. When finished, release the pressure naturally. 9. Fluff the quinoa-bean mixture with a fork and season with salt and pepper. 10. Divide the quinoa among bowls and top with the chicken and some of the cooking liquid from the pot. 11. Top the dish with the guacamole and sprinkle with the optional toppings, if using, and serve.

Per Serving: Calories 937; Fat: 65.62g; Sodium: 659mg; Carbs: 31.42g; Fibre: 8g; Sugar: 2.13g; Protein: 54.98g

Chicken Bacon Salad

⏰ Prep Time: 10 minutes   🍲 Cook: 10 minutes   ❖ Serves: 4

225g bacon
240ml water or chicken stock
680g boneless, skinless chicken breast, cut into bite-size pieces
150g cherry tomatoes, halved
115g mayonnaise
Coarse salt
Freshly ground pepper
220g spring mix lettuce

1. Select SEAR/SAUTÉ. Select Lo3, and then press START/STOP to begin cooking. 2. When the pot is hot, cook the bacon until browned and crispy, then transfer the bacon to a paper towels to drain any excess fat. Discard the drippings but do not wipe clean. 3. Add the water or chicken stock to the pot, making sure to scrape up any browned bits from the bottom. Add the chicken. 4. Close the lid, turn the pressure release valve to SEAL position, and then move the slider to PRESSURE. Select HI and set the cooking time to 6 minutes. Press START/STOP to begin cooking. When finished, release the pressure quickly. 5. Remove the chicken and allow cooling completely. 6. Mix the chicken, tomatoes and mayonnaise in a large bowl. 7. Crumble the bacon and gently fold into the chicken mixture. Season them with salt and pepper. 8. Place 55g of lettuce on each of the four plates. Evenly divide the chicken salad and place on top of the lettuce. Enjoy.

Per Serving: Calories 618; Fat: 36.52g; Sodium: 1679mg; Carbs: 50.57g; Fibre: 6g; Sugar: 15.55g; Protein: 25.28g

Pulled Turkey

⏲ **Prep Time: 20 minutes** 🍲 **Cook: 30 minutes** 🍽 **Serves: 6**

1 tablespoon lemon pepper seasoning blend
1135g boneless turkey tenderloins
160ml chicken broth
50g ginger jam
2 tablespoons fresh lemon juice
2 tablespoons red wine vinegar
2 tablespoons packed fresh oregano leaves, minced
½ teaspoon red pepper flakes

1. Pat and massage the lemon pepper seasoning into the turkey tenderloins. 2. Mix the broth, jam, lemon juice, vinegar, oregano, and red pepper flakes in the pot until the jam dissolves into the sauce. 3. Place the turkey tenderloins into this sauce without turning the meat over. 4. Close the lid, turn the pressure release valve to SEAL position, and then move the slider to PRESSURE. Select HI and set the cooking time to 25 minutes. Press START/STOP to begin cooking. When finished, release the pressure naturally. 5. Shred the meat with two forks in the pot, and then stir well to coat with sauce. Let rest for 5 to 10 minutes to blend the flavours and allow the meat to continue to absorb the sauce. 6. Serve and enjoy.

Per Serving: Calories 961; Fat: 85.93g; Sodium: 195mg; Carbs: 1.87g; Fibre: 0.3g; Sugar: 0.4g; Protein: 41.96g

Pasta Chicken Puttanesca

⏲ **Prep Time: 20 minutes** 🍲 **Cook: 10 minutes** 🍽 **Serves: 4**

2 small (170g to 200g) boneless, skinless chicken breasts
Salt and freshly ground black pepper
2 tablespoons olive oil
345g dry penne pasta
600ml store-bought chicken or vegetable broth, or homemade
1 (415g) can diced tomatoes with Italian herbs, with juices
65g oil-cured black or Kalamata olives
4 oil-packed rolled anchovies with capers, plus 1 tablespoon oil from the jar
Pinch of red pepper flakes

1. Pat the chicken dry with paper towels. Season the chicken all over with salt and several grinds of pepper. 2. Select SEAR/SAUTÉ. Select Lo3, and then press START/STOP to begin cooking. 3. When the pot is hot, heat the oil; add the chicken breasts and cook them for 3 minutes on each side until golden brown. 4. Stop the process, and add penne, broth, tomatoes, olives, anchovies and oil, red pepper flakes, and several grinds of pepper. Stir everything together and place the chicken breasts on top of the pasta mixture. 5. Close the lid, turn the pressure release valve to SEAL position, and then move the slider to PRESSURE. Select LO and set the cooking time to 6 minutes. Press START/STOP to begin cooking. When finished, release the pressure quickly. 6. Transfer the chicken to a cutting board and chop it into bite-size pieces. Return the chicken to the pot and stir to combine. 7. Loosely cover the pot with the lid and let stand for 5 minutes; the liquid will thicken upon standing. Enjoy.

Per Serving: Calories 974; Fat: 61.53g; Sodium: 1354mg; Carbs: 96.66g; Fibre: 13.1g; Sugar: 3.83g; Protein: 14.65g

Korean Chicken Wings

⏱ **Prep Time: 10 minutes** 🍲 **Cook: 45 minutes** ❖ **Serves: 4**

Wings:
1 teaspoon pepper
1 teaspoon salt
910g chicken wings

Sauce:
2 packets Splenda
1 tablespoon minced garlic
1 tablespoon minced ginger
1 tablespoon sesame oil
1 teaspoon agave nectar
1 tablespoon mayo
2 tablespoon gochujang

Finishing:
40g chopped green onions
2 teaspoon sesame seeds

1. Place the Cook & Crisp Basket in your Pressure Cooker Steam Fryer. 2. Line the Cook & Crisp Basket with foil. 3. Season the chicken wings with black pepper and salt and place in the Cook & Crisp Basket. 4. Put on the Smart Lid on top of the Ninja Foodi Steam Fryer. 5. Move the Lid Slider to the "Air Fry/Stovetop". Select the "Air Fry" mode for cooking. 6. Adjust the cooking temperature to 200°C. 7. Air fry the seasoned chicken wings for around 20 minutes, turning at 10 minutes. 8. As chicken wings air fries, mix all the sauce components. 9. Once a thermometer says that the chicken has reached 70°C, take out wings and place into a suitable bowl. 10. Add half of the prepared sauce mixture over wings, tossing well to coat. 11. Put coated wings back into Pressure Cooker Steam Fryer for around 5 minutes or till they reach 75°C. 12. Remove and sprinkle with green onions and sesame seeds. Dip into extra sauce.

Per serving: Calories: 489; Fat: 11g; Sodium: 501mg; Carbs: 8.9g; Fibre: 4.6g; Sugar 8g; Protein 26g

Chicken Fajita Rollups

⏱ **Prep Time: 10 minutes** 🍲 **Cook: 12 minutes** ❖ **Serves: 6-8**

½ teaspoon oregano
½ teaspoon cayenne pepper
1 teaspoon cumin
1 teaspoon garlic powder
2 teaspoons paprika
½ sliced red onion
½ yellow bell pepper, sliced into strips
½ green bell pepper, sliced into strips
½ red bell pepper, sliced into strips
3 chicken breasts

1. Place the Cook & Crisp Basket in your Pressure Cooker Steam Fryer. 2. Mix oregano, cayenne pepper, garlic powder, cumin and paprika along with a pinch or two of pepper and salt. Set to the side. 3. Slice chicken breasts lengthwise into 2 slices. 4. Between two pieces of parchment paper, add breast slices and pound till they are ¼-inch thick. With seasoning, liberally season both sides of chicken slices. 5. Put 2 strips of each color of bell pepper and a few onion slices onto chicken pieces. 6. Roll up tightly and secure with toothpicks. 7. Repeat with remaining ingredients and sprinkle and rub mixture that is left over the chicken rolls. 8. Grease your Ninja Foodi Pressure Steam Fryer basket and place 3 rollups into the fryer. 9. Put on the Smart Lid on top of the Ninja Foodi Steam Fryer. 10. Move the Lid Slider to the "Air Fry/Stovetop". Select the "Air Fry" mode for cooking. 11. Cook 12 minutes at 200°C. 12. Repeat with remaining rollups. 13. Serve with salad!

Per serving: Calories: 372; Fat: 20g; Sodium: 891mg; Carbs: 29g; Fibre: 3g; Sugar 8g; Protein 7g

Turkey Breast with Mustard-Maple Glaze

⏲ **Prep Time: 10 minutes** 🍲 **Cook: 30 minutes** 🍽 **Serves: 5-7**

1 tablespoon vegan butter
1 tablespoon stone-brown mustard
60g pure maple syrup
1 teaspoon crushed pepper
2 teaspoon salt
½ teaspoon dried rosemary
2 minced garlic cloves
60ml olive oil
1135g turkey breast loin

1. Place the Cook & Crisp Basket in your Pressure Cooker Steam Fryer. 2. Mix pepper, salt, rosemary, garlic, and olive oil together. Spread herb mixture over turkey breast. Cover and chill 2 hours or overnight to marinade. 3. Make sure to remove from fridge about half an hour before cooking. 4. Place loin into the basket. Put on the Smart Lid on top of the Ninja Foodi Steam Fryer. Move the Lid Slider to the "Air Fry/Stovetop". Select the "Air Fry" mode for cooking. 5. Adjust the cooking temperature to 200°C. Cook for 20 minutes. 6. While turkey cooks, melt butter in the microwave. Then add brown mustard and maple syrup. 7. Spoon on butter mixture over turkey. Cook another 10 minutes. 8. Remove turkey from the Pressure Cooker Steam Fryer and let rest 5 to 10 minutes before attempting to slice. 9. Slice against the grain and enjoy!

Per serving: Calories: 372; Fat: 20g; Sodium: 891mg; Carbs: 29g; Fibre: 3g; Sugar 8g; Protein 27g

Crispy Oats Crusted Chicken Drumsticks

⏲ **Prep Time: 10 minutes** 🍲 **Cook: 20 minutes** 🍽 **Serves: 4**

1 teaspoon cayenne pepper
2 tablespoon mustard powder
2 tablespoon oregano
2 tablespoon thyme
3 tablespoon coconut milk
1 beaten egg
25g cauliflower
20g gluten-free oats
8 chicken drumsticks

1. Place the Cook & Crisp Basket in your Pressure Cooker Steam Fryer. 2. Lay out chicken and season with pepper and salt on all sides. 3. Add all other ingredients except the egg and coconut milk to a blender, blending till a smooth-like breadcrumb mixture is created. Place in a suitable bowl and add a beaten egg and coconut milk to another bowl, whisk well. 4. Dip chicken into breadcrumbs, then into egg, and breadcrumbs once more. 5. Place coated drumsticks into basket. Put on the Smart Lid on top of the Ninja Foodi Steam Fryer. Move the Lid Slider to the "Air Fry/Stovetop". Select the "Air Fry" mode for cooking. 6. Adjust the cooking temperature to 175°C. 7. Cook for 20 minutes. Bump up the temperature to 200°C. Cook for another 5 minutes till crispy.

Per serving: Calories: 489; Fat: 11g; Sodium: 501mg; Carbs: 8.9g; Fibre: 4.6g; Sugar 8g; Protein 26g

Delicious Chicken Mushroom Kabobs

⏱ **Prep Time: 10 minutes** 🍲 **Cook: 20 minutes** ❖ **Serves: 4**

2 diced chicken breasts
3 bell peppers
6 mushrooms
Sesame seeds
80ml low-sodium soy sauce
90g raw honey
Olive oil
Salt and pepper, to taste

1. Place the Cook & Crisp Basket in your Pressure Cooker Steam Fryer. 2. Chop up chicken into cubes, seasoning with a few sprays of olive oil, pepper, and salt. 3. Dice up bell peppers and cut mushrooms in half. 4. Mix soy sauce and honey till well mixed. Add sesame seeds and stir. 5. Skewer chicken, peppers, and mushrooms onto wooden skewers. 6. Coat kabobs with honey-soy sauce. 7. Place coated kabobs in "cook & crisp basket". Put on the Smart Lid on top of the Ninja Foodi Steam Fryer. Move the Lid Slider to the "Air Fry/Stovetop". Select the "Air Fry" mode for cooking. 8. Adjust the cooking temperature to 200°C. Cook for 15 to 20 minutes.

Per serving: Calories: 219; Fat: 10g; Sodium: 891mg; Carbs: 22.9g; Fibre: 4g; Sugar 4g; Protein 13g

Juicy Chicken Thighs

⏱ **Prep Time: 15 minutes** 🍲 **Cook: 25 minutes** ❖ **Serves: 4**

240ml water or chicken stock
1400g chicken thighs, skin on
240ml fresh orange juice
180g ketchup
1 tbsp. (15ml) Worcestershire sauce
2 tbsp. (30g) light brown sugar
2 tsp. (10ml) white wine vinegar
2 tsp. (10ml) hot sauce
20g chopped fresh cilantro

1. Pour the water or chicken stock into the pot, and then add the chicken thighs. 2. Close the lid, turn the pressure release valve to SEAL position, and then move the slider to PRESSURE. Select HI and set the cooking time to 9 minutes. Press START/STOP to begin cooking. When finished, release the pressure quickly. 3. Remove the chicken from the pot and place on a baking pan. 4. Clean the pot. Place the rack in the pot in the higher broil position and then place the pan on it. Close the lid and move slider to AIR FRY/STOVETOP, then use the dial to select BROIL. Set the cooking time to 5 minutes and then press START/STOP to begin cooking. 5. Clean the pot and wipe clean. Select SEAR/SAUTÉ. Select Hi5, and then press START/STOP to begin cooking. 6. When the pot is hot, add orange juice, ketchup, Worcestershire sauce, brown sugar, vinegar and hot sauce, bring to a liquid and then simmer the sauce at Lo1 for 7 to 8 minutes until thick and slightly reduced. 7. Pour the sauce over the chicken thighs in the plate, sprinkle them with cilantro and enjoy.

Per Serving: Calories 877; Fat: 57.04g; Sodium: 860mg; Carbs: 31.26g; Fibre: 0.5g; Sugar: 22.21g; Protein: 57.74g

Chapter 4 Poultry Mains

Chapter 5 Seafood Mains

46 Potato Salmon Fish Cakes
46 Lemon Cajun Salmon
47 Coconut Shrimp
47 Prawns and Ear Corn Boil
48 Spiced Fish Tacos
48 Honey–Soy Braised Salmon
49 Pesto Tilapia with Creamy Sun–Dried Tomatoes Sauce
49 Crab Legs with Butter & Lemon Wedges
50 Roasted Salmon with Capers–Yogurt Dressing
50 Asian Style Sea Bass
51 Crunchy Fish Fingers
51 Parmesan Tilapia Fillets
52 Salmon Croquettes
52 Salmon with Courgette & Cherry Tomatoes

Potato Salmon Fish Cakes

⏰ **Prep Time: 10 minutes**   🍲 **Cook: 8 minutes | Serves: 4**

400g of potatoes, boiled and mashed
285g cooked salmon, flaked
1 teaspoon olive oil
30g almond flour
1 handful parsley, fresh, chopped
1 handful of capers
1 teaspoon lemon zest

1. Place the Cook & Crisp Basket in your Pressure Cooker Steam Fryer. 2. Brush salmon with olive oil. Place the potatoes, flaked salmon, lemon zest, parsley, and capers in a suitable bowl and mix well. Make 4 large cakes out of the mixture. Dust fish cakes with flour. Place them in the fridge for an hour. Add salmon cakes to the Cook & Crisp Basket. Put on the Smart Lid on top of the Ninja Foodi Steam Fryer. Move the Lid Slider to the "Air Fry/Stovetop". Select the "Air Fry" mode for cooking. 3. Adjust the cooking temperature to 175°C. Cook for around 8 minutes. Serve warm.

Per serving: Calories 303; Fat: 10.4g; Sodium 703mg; Carbs: 9.2g; Fibre: 0g; Sugars 8.7g; Protein 40.6g

Lemon Cajun Salmon

⏰ **Prep Time: 10 minutes**   🍲 **Cook: 7 minutes**   ❖ **Serves: 1**

1 salmon fillet
1 teaspoon Cajun seasoning
2 lemon wedges, for serving
1 teaspoon liquid stevia
½ lemon, juiced

1. Place the Cook & Crisp Basket in your Pressure Cooker Steam Fryer. 2. Mix lemon juice and liquid stevia and coat salmon with this mixture. Sprinkle Cajun seasoning all over salmon. Place salmon on parchment paper in the Cook & Crisp Basket. Put on the Smart Lid on top of the Ninja Foodi Steam Fryer. Move the Lid Slider to the "Air Fry/Stovetop". Select the "Air Fry" mode for cooking. Adjust the cooking temperature to 175°C. Cook for around 7-minutes. Serve with lemon wedges.

Per serving: Calories 570; Fat: 29.3g; Sodium 845mg; Carbs: 5.8g; Fibre: 1.6g; Sugars 2.7g; Protein 68.6g

| Chapter 5 Seafood Mains

Coconut Shrimp

⏱ **Prep Time: 10 minutes** 🍲 **Cook: 20 minutes** ⚑ **Serves: 2**

55g breadcrumbs
Salt and black pepper to taste
30g shredded coconut, unsweetened
½ teaspoon cayenne pepper
240ml coconut milk
8 large shrimps
1 tablespoon sugar-free syrup
¼ teaspoon hot sauce
135g orange jam, sugar-free
1 teaspoon mustard

1. Place the Cook & Crisp Basket in your Pressure Cooker Steam Fryer. 2. Place breadcrumbs, coconut, salt, pepper, and cayenne pepper in a suitable bowl and mix. Dip the shrimp in coconut milk first, then in breadcrumb mixture. Line baking sheet and arrange shrimp on it. Place in the Cook & Crisp Basket. Put on the Smart Lid on top of the Ninja Foodi Steam Fryer. Move the Lid Slider to the "Air Fry/Stovetop". Select the "Air Fry" mode for cooking. Put on the Smart Lid on top of the Ninja Foodi Steam Fryer. 3. Move the Lid Slider to the "Air Fry/Stovetop". Select the "Air Fry" mode for cooking. 4. Adjust the cooking temperature to 175°C. Cook for around 20 minutes. Mix the orange jam, mustard, syrup, and hot sauce. Add the shrimp to a serving platter and drizzle with sauce and serve.

Per serving: Calories 459; Fat: 3.6g; Sodium 1614mg; Carbs: 82g; Fibre: 11.5g; Sugars 8.3g; Protein 25.9g

Prawns and Ear Corn Boil

⏱ **Prep Time: 5 minutes** 🍲 **Cook: 15 minutes** ⚑ **Serves: 4**

240 ml chicken stock
1 teaspoon minced garlic
2 medium red potatoes, quartered
1 medium ear corn, husked
1 (75 g) link andouille sausage, cut into 4 pieces on the bias
½ tablespoon Old Bay seasoning
110 g peeled and deveined extra-large prawns
3 tablespoons butter, melted
½ medium lemon, for serving
1 tablespoon chopped fresh parsley

1. Add stock and garlic to the pot and then place in the rack. 2. Add potatoes, corn, and sausage, and then sprinkle Old Bay seasoning over everything. 3. Close the lid, turn the pressure release valve to SEAL position, and then move the slider to PRESSURE. Select HI and set the cooking time to 3 minutes. Press START/STOP to begin cooking. When finished, release the pressure quickly. 4. Add prawns, stir, then immediately replace the lid and wait for 5 to 8 minutes until the prawns is pink and cooked through. 5. To serve, remove everything to a large bowl and serve with a side of butter, lemon, and sprinkle of parsley.

Per Serving: Calories 398; Fat: 18.34g; Sodium: 688mg; Carbs: 40.89g; Fibre: 5.3g; Sugar: 3.7g; Protein: 20.13g

Spiced Fish Tacos

⏰ **Prep Time: 15 minutes** 🍲 **Cook: 5 minutes** 🔖 **Serves: 4**

½ tablespoon olive oil
½ teaspoon minced garlic
⅛ teaspoon smoked paprika
⅛ teaspoon chilli powder
⅛ teaspoon ground cumin
¼ teaspoon salt
⅛ teaspoon Cajun seasoning
2 (110g) frozen tilapia fillets
240ml water

Spicy Lime Crema:
2 tablespoons sour cream
1 tablespoon mayonnaise
1 teaspoon lime juice
⅛ teaspoon garlic salt
⅛ teaspoon salt
½ teaspoon sriracha sauce

For Serving:
3 small tortillas, warmed
30g shredded cabbage
1 ½ tablespoons pico de gallo
1 tablespoon chopped coriander
½ medium lime

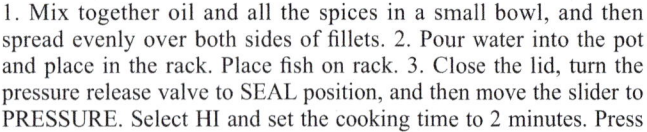

1. Mix together oil and all the spices in a small bowl, and then spread evenly over both sides of fillets. 2. Pour water into the pot and place in the rack. Place fish on rack. 3. Close the lid, turn the pressure release valve to SEAL position, and then move the slider to PRESSURE. Select HI and set the cooking time to 2 minutes. Press START/STOP to begin cooking. When finished, release the pressure quickly. 4. Carefully transfer fish to a small bowl. 5. In a separate small bowl, combine all Spicy Lime Crema ingredients and refrigerate until ready to use. 6. To serve, transfer tortillas to a serving plate. Evenly break up the fish between tortillas. Top the dish with cabbage, pico de gallo, Spicy Lime Crema, coriander, and a squeeze of lime.

Per Serving: Calories 209; Fat: 7.42g; Sodium: 584mg; Carbs: 31.21g; Fibre: 1.2g; Sugar: 11.8g; Protein: 4.92g

Honey-Soy Braised Salmon

⏰ **Prep Time: 5 minutes** 🍲 **Cook: 15 minutes** 🔖 **Serves: 2**

60 ml soy sauce
2 tablespoons honey
½ tablespoon apple cider vinegar
½ tablespoon olive oil
1½ tablespoons brown sugar
½ teaspoon minced garlic
1 (125g) frozen salmon fillet

1. Stir all of the ingredients together in the pot. 2. Close the lid, turn the pressure release valve to SEAL position, and then move the slider to PRESSURE. Select HI and set the cooking time to 3 minutes. Press START/STOP to begin cooking. When finished, release the pressure naturally. 3. Transfer the fish to a plate or bowl. 4. Cook the sauce at Hi5 on SEAR/SAUTÉ mode for 8 minutes until reduced and thickened. 5. Spoon 1 tablespoon sauce over fish and serve.

Per Serving: Calories 311; Fat: 14.26g; Sodium: 791mg; Carbs: 29.29g; Fibre: 0.7g; Sugar: 27.12g; Protein: 17.01g

Chapter 5 Seafood Mains

Pesto Tilapia with Creamy Sun-Dried Tomatoes Sauce

⏰ **Prep Time: 5 minutes** 🍲 **Cook: 5 minutes** 🍽 **Serves: 2**

1 tablespoon butter
3 tablespoons chopped sun-dried tomatoes
55 g artichoke heart quarters
1 teaspoon lemon juice
⅛ teaspoon salt
⅛ teaspoon ground black pepper
120ml chicken stock
1 tablespoon basil pesto
2 (110g) frozen tilapia fillets
2 tablespoons heavy cream
3 tablespoons shredded Parmesan cheese

1. Add butter, tomatoes, artichokes, lemon juice, salt, pepper, and stock to the pot. 2. Spread pesto all over the tops of fillets and place on the rack. Lower the rack into the pot. 3. Close the lid, turn the pressure release valve to SEAL position, and then move the slider to PRESSURE. Select HI and set the cooking time to 2 minutes. Press START/STOP to begin cooking. When finished, release the pressure quickly. 4. Carefully transfer fish to a serving plate. 5. Stir cream and Parmesan into the sauce. Ladle sauce over fish and serve.

Per Serving: Calories 387; Fat: 21.3g; Sodium: 701mg; Carbs: 30.64g; Fibre: 2.9g; Sugar: 22.45g; Protein: 20.55g

Crab Legs with Butter & Lemon Wedges

⏰ **Prep Time: 5 minutes** 🍲 **Cook: 1 minute** 🍽 **Serves: 2**

240ml water
455g crab legs
⅛ teaspoon Old Bay seasoning
2 tablespoons clarified butter
½ medium lemon cut into wedges

1. Pour water into pot and place in the rack. 2. Add crab legs and sprinkle with Old Bay seasoning. 3. Close the lid, turn the pressure release valve to SEAL position, and then move the slider to PRESSURE. Select LO and set the cooking time to 1 minute. Press START/STOP to begin cooking. When finished, release the pressure quickly. 4. Remove crab to a plate and serve with butter and lemon.

Per Serving: Calories 302; Fat: 14g; Sodium: 758mg; Carbs: 0.96g; Fibre: 0g; Sugar: 0.31g; Protein: 41.13g

Roasted Salmon with Capers-Yogurt Dressing

⏰ Prep Time: 10 minutes   🍲 Cook: 8 minutes   🍽 Serves: 2

1 teaspoon capers, chopped
2 sprigs dill, chopped
1 lemon zest
1 tablespoon olive oil
4 slices lemon
310g salmon fillet
Dressing:
5 capers, chopped
1 sprig dill, chopped
2 tablespoons plain yogurt
Pinch of lemon zest
Salt and black pepper to taste

1. Place the Cook & Crisp Basket in your Pressure Cooker Steam Fryer. 2. Mix dill, capers, lemon zest, olive oil and salt in a suitable bowl. Cover the salmon with this mixture. Put on the Smart Lid on top of the Ninja Foodi Steam Fryer. 3. Move the Lid Slider to the "Air Fry/Stovetop". Select the "Air Fry" mode for cooking. 4. Adjust the cooking temperature to 200°C. Cook salmon for around 8 minutes. Mix the dressing ingredients in another bowl. When salmon is cooked, place on serving plate and drizzle dressing over it. Place lemon slices at the side of the plate and serve.

Per serving: Calories 669; Fat: 53.8g; Sodium 905mg; Carbs: 41.7g; Fibre: 8.6g; Sugars 12.3g; Protein 14g

Asian Style Sea Bass

⏰ Prep Time: 10 minutes   🍲 Cook: 20 minutes   🍽 Serves: 2

1 medium sea bass or halibut (335g)
2 garlic cloves, minced
1 tablespoon olive oil
3 slices of ginger, julienned
2 tablespoons cooking wine
1 tomato, cut into quarters
1 lime, cut
1 green onion, chopped

1. Place the Cook & Crisp Basket in your Pressure Cooker Steam Fryer. 2. Prepare ginger, garlic oil mixture: sauté ginger and garlic with oil until golden brown in a suitable saucepan over medium-heat on top of the stove. Prepare fish: clean, rinse, and pat dry. Cut in half to fit into basket. Place the fish inside of "cook & crisp basket" then drizzle it with cooking wine. Layer tomato and lime slices on top of fish. Cover with garlic ginger oil mixture. Top with green onion. Cover with aluminium foil. Put on the Smart Lid on top of the Ninja Foodi Steam Fryer. 3. Move the Lid Slider to the "Air Fry/Stovetop". Select the "Air Fry" mode for cooking. 4. Adjust the cooking temperature to 180°C. Cook for around 20 minutes.

Per serving: Calories 105; Fat: 2.4g; Sodium 812mg; Carbs: 12.2g; Fibre: 2.4g; Sugars 2.4g; Protein 9.5g

Crunchy Fish Fingers

⏰ Prep Time: 10 minutes 🍲 Cook: 10 minutes 🍽 Serves: 2

285g codfish, sliced into strips
2 teaspoons mixed dried herbs
2 eggs
¼ teaspoon baking soda
1 teaspoon rice flour
2 teaspoons cornflower
2 tablespoons almond flour
½ lemon, juiced
1 teaspoon ginger garlic
½ teaspoon turmeric powder
½ teaspoon red chilli flakes
2 teaspoons garlic powder
2 tablespoons olive oil
110g breadcrumbs
Tartar sauce or ketchup

1. Place the Cook & Crisp Basket in your Pressure Cooker Steam Fryer. 2. Place fish fingers in a suitable bowl. Add a teaspoon of mixed herbs, 1 teaspoon of garlic powder, red chilli flakes, turmeric powder, ginger garlic, lemon juice, salt and black pepper. Stir well and set aside for around 10 minutes. In another bowl, mix almond flour, rice flour, corn flour and baking soda. Break eggs into this bowl. Stir well then add fish. Set aside for around 10 minutes. 3. Mix breadcrumbs and remaining 1 teaspoon of mixed herbs and 1 teaspoon of garlic powder. Cover fish with breadcrumb mixture. Lay aluminium foil in the Cook & Crisp Basket. Lay the fish fingers in the basket and cover with olive oil. Put on the Smart Lid on top of the Ninja Foodi Steam Fryer. 4. Move the Lid Slider to the "Air Fry/Stovetop". Select the "Air Fry" mode for cooking. 5. Adjust the cooking temperature to 180°C. Cook for around 10 minutes and serve with tartar sauce or ketchup.

Per serving: Calories 541; Fat: 12.4g; Sodium 250mg; Carbs: 85.4g; Fibre: 21.3g; Sugars 6.1g; Protein 26.5g

Parmesan Tilapia Fillets

⏰ Prep Time: 10 minutes 🍲 Cook: 5 minutes 🍽 Serves: 4

1 tablespoon olive oil
4 tilapia fillets
75g grated Parmesan cheese
1 tablespoon parsley, chopped
2 teaspoons paprika
Pinch of garlic powder

1. Place the Cook & Crisp Basket in your Pressure Cooker Steam Fryer. 2. Brush oil over tilapia fillets. Mix the remaining recipe ingredients in a suitable bowl. Coat tilapia fillets with parmesan mixture. Line the Cook & Crisp Basket with parchment paper and arrange fillets. Place in Pressure Cooker Steam Fryer. Put on the Smart Lid on top of the Ninja Foodi Steam Fryer. 3. Move the Lid Slider to the "Air Fry/Stovetop". Select the "Air Fry" mode for cooking. 4. Adjust the cooking temperature to 175°C. Cook for around 5 minutes.

Per serving: Calories 323; Fat: 17.9g; Sodium 838mg; Carbs: 4.3g; Fibre: 1.5g; Sugars 1g; Protein 35.5g

Salmon Croquettes

⏲ **Prep Time: 10 minutes**   🍲 **Cook: 10 minutes**   ❦ **Serves: 4**

400g tin of red salmon, drained
2 free-range eggs
5 tablespoons olive oil
45g breadcrumbs
2 tablespoons spring onions, chopped
Black pepper and salt to taste
Pinch of herbs

1. Place the Cook & Crisp Basket in your Pressure Cooker Steam Fryer. 2. Add drained salmon into a suitable bowl and mash well. Break in the egg, add herbs, spring onions, salt, pepper and mix well. In another bowl, mix breadcrumbs and oil and mix well. Take a spoon of the salmon mixture and shape it into a croquette shape in your hand. Roll it in the breadcrumbs and place inside the Cook & Crisp Basket. Put on the Smart Lid on top of the Ninja Foodi Steam Fryer. 3. Move the Lid Slider to the "Air Fry/Stovetop". Select the "Air Fry" mode for cooking. 4. Set your Ninja Foodi Pressure Steam Fryer to 200°C for around 10 minutes.

Per serving: Calories 419; Fat: 15.8g; Sodium 3342mg; Carbs: 0.4g; Fibre: 0.2g; Sugars 0g; Protein 65.4g

Salmon with Courgette & Cherry Tomatoes

⏲ **Prep Time: 10 minutes**   🍲 **Cook: 10 minutes.** |**Serves: 2**

2 (170g) salmon fillets, skin on
Black pepper and salt to taste
1 teaspoon olive oil
2 large courgettes, trimmed and spiralised
1 avocado, peeled and chopped
Small handful of parsley, chopped
½ garlic clove, minced
Small handful cherry tomatoes, halved
Small handful of black olives, chopped
2 tablespoons pine nuts, toasted

1. Place the Cook & Crisp Basket in your Pressure Cooker Steam Fryer. 2. Brush salmon with olive oil and season with black pepper and salt. Place salmon in the Cook & Crisp Basket. Put on the Smart Lid on top of the Ninja Foodi Steam Fryer. Move the Lid Slider to the "Air Fry/Stovetop". Select the "Air Fry" mode for cooking. Adjust the cooking temperature to 175°C. Cook for around 10 minutes. Blend the avocado, garlic, and parsley in a food processor until smooth. Toss in a suitable bowl with courgette, olives, and tomatoes. Divide vegetables between two plates, top each portion with salmon fillet, sprinkle with pine nuts, and serve.

Per serving: Calories 609; Fat: 19.5g; Sodium 132mg; Carbs: 49g; Fibre: 6g; Sugars 13.3g; Protein 57.5g

Chapter 5 Seafood Mains

Chapter 6 Beef, Pork, and Lamb

- 54 London Broil with Garlic Butter
- 54 Flavourful Beef with Carrots
- 55 Lemony Lamb with Chickpea & Pitas
- 55 Pork Chops with Bacon & Cream Sauce
- 56 BBQ Beef Brisket
- 56 Bourbon Barbecue Pork Ribs
- 57 Lamb and Wheat Berries Stew
- 57 Beef Pot with Potatoes and Carrots
- 58 BBQ Beef Cheeseburgers
- 58 Easy Air Fried Flank Steak
- 59 Herb–Garlic Fillet Mignon
- 59 Beef Meatloaf Cups with Tomato Sauce Glaze
- 60 Ribeye Steak with Blue Cheese
- 60 Savoury Rump Roast

London Broil with Garlic Butter

⏰ Prep Time: 10 minutes 🍲 Cook: 28 minutes 🍽 Serves: 4

680g London broil
Salt and black pepper, to taste
¼ teaspoon bay leaf
3 tablespoons butter, cold
1 tablespoon Dijon mustard
1 teaspoon garlic, pressed
1 tablespoon fresh parsley, chopped

1. Place the Cook & Crisp Basket in your Pressure Cooker Steam Fryer. 2. Toss the beef with the salt and black pepper; brush the basket with oil and place the beef in it. 3. Put on the Smart Lid on top of the Ninja Foodi Steam Fryer. 4. Move the Lid Slider to the "Air Fry/Stovetop". Select the "Air Fry" mode for cooking. 5. Cook the beef at 200°C for around 28 minutes, turning over halfway through the cooking time. 6. In the meantime, mix the butter with the remaining recipe ingredients and place it in the refrigerator until well-chilled. 7. Serve warm beef with the chilled garlic butter on the side. Serve.

Per serving: Calories: 394; Fat:17.5g; Carbs: 26.5g; Fibre: 1.3g; Sugars: 6.4g; Proteins: 32.5g

Flavourful Beef with Carrots

⏰ Prep Time: 10 minutes 🍲 Cook: 55 minutes 🍽 Serves: 5

910g top sirloin roast
2 tablespoons olive oil
Sea salt and black pepper, to taste
2 carrots, sliced
1 tablespoon fresh coriander
1 tablespoon fresh thyme
1 tablespoon fresh rosemary

1. Place the Cook & Crisp Basket in your Pressure Cooker Steam Fryer. 2. Toss the beef with the olive oil, salt, and black pepper; place the beef in the Cook & Crisp Basket Put on the Smart Lid on top of the Ninja Foodi Steam Fryer. 3. Move the Lid Slider to the "Air Fry/Stovetop". Select the "Air Fry" mode for cooking. 4. Cook the beef eye round cook at 200°C for around 45 minutes, turning it over halfway through the cooking time. 5. Top the beef with the carrots and herbs. Continue to cook an additional 10 minutes. 6. Enjoy!

Per serving: Calories 349; Fat: 15.1g; Sodium 157mg; Carbs: 25.6g; Fibre: 2.6g; Sugars 22.5g; Protein 29.7g

| Chapter 6 Beef, Pork, and Lamb

Lemony Lamb with Chickpea & Pitas

⏰ **Prep Time: 15 minutes** 🍲 **Cook: 25 minutes** 🍽 **Serves: 4-6**

1 tbsp. (15ml) extra-virgin olive oil
4 (115g) bone-in lamb shoulder chops
Salt
Freshly ground black pepper
1 yellow onion, diced
½ tsp. ground fennel seeds
1 tsp. smoked paprika
½ tsp. dried oregano
¼ tsp. crushed red pepper flakes
½ lemon
2 (440g) cans chickpeas, drained and rinsed
175ml chicken or beef stock
1 (410g) can fire-roasted diced tomatoes
1 (170g) can tomato paste
12 (7 inches) pitas
Tzatziki, for serving (optional)

1. Select SEAR/SAUTÉ. Select Lo3, and then press START/STOP to begin cooking. 2. When the pot is hot, heat the oil; add the lamb and season the top side with salt and black pepper, and then sear the first side for 3 to 4 minutes; flip the lamb and season that top side with salt and black pepper, then add the onion and sauté for 2 more minutes. Add the fennel, more salt and black pepper, paprika, oregano, red pepper flakes and lemon half to the pot. Stir everything to combine. 3. Stop the process, and stir in the chickpeas, stock and diced tomatoes. 4. Close the lid, turn the pressure release valve to SEAL position, and then move the slider to PRESSURE. Select HI and set the cooking time to 15 minutes. Press START/STOP to begin cooking. When finished, release the pressure quickly. 5. Transfer the lamb chops to a cutting board, then remove the bones and dice the meat. 6. Return the meat to the pot. Squeeze out the juice from the lemon half and discard the half. 7. Stir in the tomato paste and adjust the salt and black pepper, if needed. Serve with pita bread and tzatziki drizzled on top, if desired.

Per Serving: Calories 366; Fat: 7.21g; Sodium: 715mg; Carbs: 62.6g; Fibre: 12.9g; Sugar: 10.73g; Protein: 18.09g

Pork Chops with Bacon & Cream Sauce

⏰ **Prep Time: 15 minutes** 🍲 **Cook: 25 minutes** 🍽 **Serves: 4**

5 strips bacon
4 (1 inch thick) bone-in pork chops
240ml chicken stock
4 tbsp. (55g) unsalted butter
1 (30g) packet dried ranch seasoning mix
115g cream cheese, softened
115g sour cream

1. Select SEAR/SAUTÉ. Select Lo3, and then press START/STOP to begin cooking. 2. When the pot is hot, add bacon and cook until browned and crispy, and then transfer them to paper towels to drain any excess fat. 3. Add the pork chops to the drippings in the pot and brown on both sides. Remove the chops and set aside. 4. Stop the process and pour the chicken stock into the pot, ensuring to scrape up any browned bits from the bottom. Return the pork chops to the pot, then add the butter and ranch seasoning. 5. Close the lid, turn the pressure release valve to SEAL position, and then move the slider to PRESSURE. Select HI and set the cooking time to 20 minutes. Press START/STOP to begin cooking. When finished, release the pressure naturally. 6. Remove the pork chops and place on a serving platter. 7. Add the cream cheese and sour cream to the pot and stir well. Season them and then pour the sauce over the pork chops. 8. Crumble the bacon and sprinkle over the top. Serve.

Per Serving: Calories 818; Fat: 44.52g; Sodium: 1082mg; Carbs: 7.43g; Fibre: 1.5g; Sugar: 2.39g; Protein: 92.84g

BBQ Beef Brisket

⏰ Prep Time: 10 minutes 🍲 Cook: 1 hour 10 minutes 🍥 Serves: 4

680g beef brisket
285g barbecue sauce
2 tablespoons soy sauce

1. Place the Cook & Crisp Basket in your Pressure Cooker Steam Fryer. 2. Toss the beef with the remaining ingredients; place the beef in the Cook & Crisp Basket. 3. Put on the Smart Lid on top of the Ninja Foodi Steam Fryer. 4. Move the Lid Slider to the "Air Fry/Stovetop". Select the "Air Fry" mode for cooking. 5. Cook the beef at 200°C for around 15 minutes, turn the beef over and turn the temperature to 180°C. 6. Continue to cook the beef for around 55 minutes more. Serve.

Per serving: Calories 319; Fat: 15.6g; Sodium 99mg; Carbs: 4.8g; Fibre: 0.7g; Sugars 2.9g; Protein 38.5g

Bourbon Barbecue Pork Ribs

⏰ Prep Time: 5 minutes 🍲 Cook: 25 minutes 🍥 Serves: 2

1 rack baby back ribs
Kosher salt
Freshly ground black pepper
45g barbecue meat rub (optional)
240ml water
1 tablespoon liquid smoke (optional)
60ml bourbon
285g classic barbecue sauce

1. Remove the membrane from the back of the ribs and cut the rack into four equal pieces if needed. Season generously with salt, pepper, and your favourite barbecue meat rub (if using). 2. Put the ribs in the pot. Add the beef stock and liquid smoke (if using). 3. Close the lid, turn the pressure release valve to SEAL position, and then move the slider to PRESSURE. Select HI and set the cooking time to 25 minutes. Press START/STOP to begin cooking. When finished, release the pressure naturally. 4. Line a baking pan with aluminium foil. 5. Mix the bourbon and barbecue sauce in a small bowl. 6. Transfer the cooked ribs to the prepared baking pan. Brush the bourbon-barbecue sauce all over the ribs, including the bones. 7. Place the baking pan in the pot. Close the lid and move slider to AIR FRY/STOVETOP, then use the dial to select BAKE/ROAST. Adjust the cooking temperature to 200°C and set the cooking time to 12 minutes. Press START/STOP to begin cooking. 8. Flip the food halfway through. 9. Brush the remaining sauce on the ribs before serving.

Per Serving: Calories 1143; Fat: 62.65g; Sodium: 1780mg; Carbs: 63.3g; Fibre: 3.2g; Sugar: 47.53g; Protein: 82.33g

| Chapter 6 Beef, Pork, and Lamb

Lamb and Wheat Berries Stew

⏱ **Prep Time: 20 minutes**   🍲 **Cook: 60 minutes**   ❖ **Serves: 6**

95g dried wheat berries, preferably soft white wheat berries
55g (½ stick) butter
1135g boneless lamb shoulder, any chunks of fat removed, the meat cut into 2-inch pieces
1 large yellow onion, chopped (190g)
600ml chicken broth
60g chopped pecans
2 teaspoons dried sage
½ teaspoon red pepper flakes
½ teaspoon table salt

1. Soak the wheat berries in a big bowl of water for at least 8 hours or up to 12 hours. Drain using a fine-mesh sieve or a small-holed colander placed in the sink. 2. Select SEAR/SAUTÉ. Select Lo3, and then press START/STOP to begin cooking. 3. When the pot is hot, melt 2 tablespoons butter; add about half the lamb pieces and brown them for 8 minutes, turning and rearranging occasionally. Transfer these to a nearby bowl, add the remaining 2 tablespoons butter, and brown the remainder of the lamb in the same way before transferring the pieces to the bowl. 4. Add the onion to the pot and cook for 4 minutes until softened; pour in the broth and scrape up any browned bits on the pot's bottom. 5. Stop the process, and stir in the soaked wheat berries, as well as the pecans, sage, red pepper flakes, and salt. Return the lamb pieces and any of the juices in their bowl to the pot. 6. Close the lid, turn the pressure release valve to SEAL position, and then move the slider to PRESSURE. Select HI and set the cooking time to 40 minutes. Press START/STOP to begin cooking. When finished, release the pressure naturally. 7. Stir the dish well before serving.

Per Serving: Calories 622; Fat: 35.42g; Sodium: 792mg; Carbs: 14.1g; Fibre: 3g; Sugar: 1.22g; Protein: 62.36g

Beef Pot with Potatoes and Carrots

⏱ **Prep Time: 20 minutes**   🍲 **Cook: 60 minutes**   ❖ **Serves: 2**

1 tablespoon oil
680g lean beef shoulder roast, trimmed
Kosher salt
Freshly ground black pepper
1 medium onion, chopped
3 garlic cloves, crushed
2 large carrots, peeled and chopped
340g fingerling potatoes
480ml beef stock
1 tablespoon Worcestershire sauce
1 tablespoon cornstarch
Fresh thyme, for garnish

1. Season the roast with salt and pepper. 2. Select SEAR/SAUTÉ. Select Lo3, and then press START/STOP to begin cooking. 3. When the pot is hot, heat the oil, and then sear the roast for 3 to 4 minutes on each side. 4. Stop the process, arrange the onion, garlic, carrots, and potatoes around the roast, and then pour in the stock and add the Worcestershire sauce. 5. Close the lid, turn the pressure release valve to SEAL position, and then move the slider to PRESSURE. Select HI and set the cooking time to 60 minutes. Press START/STOP to begin cooking. When finished, release the pressure naturally. 6. Transfer the roast and vegetables to a serving platter. Let rest while you make the gravy. 7. Strain the beef stock into a bowl, discarding the fat solids. 8. Return all but 2 tablespoons of the stock to the pot and select SEAR/SAUTÉ. Whisk the cornstarch into the reserved stock in the bowl, then stir the slurry into the pot and bring to a simmer at Lo2 for 5 minutes until thickened, stirring often. 9. Taste and season with more salt, pepper, or Worcestershire sauce if desired. Pour the gravy into a gravy boat. 10. Serve the pot roast and veggies with the gravy and garnish with fresh thyme.

Per Serving: Calories 846; Fat: 27.5g; Sodium: 1426mg; Carbs: 48.64g; Fibre: 6.8g; Sugar: 7.97g; Protein: 96.64g

BBQ Beef Cheeseburgers

⏰ **Prep Time: 10 minutes** 🍲 **Cook: 15 minutes** ❖ **Serves: 3**

315g chuck
1 teaspoon garlic, minced
2 tablespoons BBQ sauce
Sea salt and black pepper, to taste
3 slices cheese
3 hamburger buns

1. Place the Cook & Crisp Basket in your Pressure Cooker Steam Fryer. 2. Mix the chuck, garlic, BBQ sauce, salt, and black pepper until everything is well mixed. Form the mixture into four patties. 3. Put on the Smart Lid on top of the Ninja Foodi Steam Fryer. 4. Move the Lid Slider to the "Air Fry/Stovetop". Select the "Air Fry" mode for cooking. 5. Cook the burgers at 195°C for about 15 minutes or until cooked through; make sure to turn them over halfway through the cooking time. 6. Top each burger with cheese. Serve your burgers on the prepared buns and enjoy!

Per serving: Calories 182; Fat: 14.1g; Sodium 18mg; Carbs: 8.9g; Fibre: 4.1g; Sugars 4g; Protein 7.2g

Easy Air Fried Flank Steak

⏰ **Prep Time: 10 minutes** 🍲 **Cook: 12 minutes** ❖ **Serves: 5**

910g flank steak
2 tablespoons olive oil
1 teaspoon paprika
Sea salt and black pepper, to taste

1. Place the Cook & Crisp Basket in your Pressure Cooker Steam Fryer. 2. Toss the steak with the remaining ingredients; place the steak in the Cook & Crisp Basket. 3. Put on the Smart Lid on top of the Ninja Foodi Steam Fryer. 4. Move the Lid Slider to the "Air Fry/Stovetop". Select the "Air Fry" mode for cooking. 5. Cook the steak at 200°C for around 12 minutes, turning over halfway through the cooking time. 6. Serve.

Per serving: Calories: 299; Fat:14.5g; Carbs: 0.3g; Fibre: 0.2g; Sugars: 0g; Proteins: 38.5g

| Chapter 6 Beef, Pork, and Lamb

Herb-Garlic Fillet Mignon

⏰ **Prep Time: 10 minutes** 🍲 **Cook: 14 minutes** 🍽 **Serves: 4**

680g fillet mignon
Sea salt and black pepper, to taste
2 tablespoons olive oil
1 teaspoon dried rosemary
1 teaspoon dried thyme
1 teaspoon dried basil
2 cloves garlic, minced

1. Place the Cook & Crisp Basket in your Pressure Cooker Steam Fryer. 2. Toss the beef with the remaining ingredients; place the beef in the Cook & Crisp Basket. 3. Put on the Smart Lid on top of the Ninja Foodi Steam Fryer. 4. Move the Lid Slider to the "Air Fry/Stovetop". Select the "Air Fry" mode for cooking. 5. Cook the beef at 200°C for around 14 minutes, turning it over halfway through the cooking time. 6. Enjoy!

Per serving: Calories: 385; Fat:26g; Carbs: 2.2g; Fibre: 0.3g; Sugars: 0.5g; Proteins: 36.2g

Beef Meatloaf Cups with Tomato Sauce Glaze

⏰ **Prep Time: 10 minutes** 🍲 **Cook: 25 minutes** 🍽 **Serves: 4**

Meatloaves:
455g ground beef
20g seasoned breadcrumbs
25g parmesan cheese, grated
1 small onion, minced
2 garlic cloves, pressed
1 egg, beaten
Sea salt and black pepper, to taste
Glaze:
4 tablespoons tomato sauce
1 tablespoon brown sugar
1 tablespoon Dijon mustard

1. Place the Cook & Crisp Basket in your Pressure Cooker Steam Fryer. 2. Mix all the recipe ingredients for the meatloaves until everything is well mixed. 3. Scrape the beef mixture into oiled silicone cups and transfer them to the Cook & Crisp Basket. 4. Put on the Smart Lid on top of the Ninja Foodi Steam Fryer. 5. Move the Lid Slider to the "Air Fry/Stovetop". Select the "Air Fry" mode for cooking. 6. Cook the beef cups at 195°C for around 20 minutes. 7. In the meantime, mix the remaining recipe ingredients for the glaze. Then, spread the glaze on top of each muffin; continue to cook for another 5 minutes. 8. Serve.

Per serving: Calories: 355; Fat:18.6g; Carbs: 14.2g; Fibre: 2.3g; Sugars: 6.2g; Proteins: 27.5g

Ribeye Steak with Blue Cheese

⏲ **Prep Time: 10 minutes** 🍲 **Cook: 15 minutes** ❖ **Serves: 4**

455g ribeye steak, bone-in
Sea salt and black pepper, to taste
2 tablespoons olive oil
½ teaspoon onion powder
1 teaspoon garlic powder
110g blue cheese, crumbled

1. Place the Cook & Crisp Basket in your Pressure Cooker Steam Fryer. 2. Toss the ribeye steak with the salt, black pepper, olive oil, onion powder, and garlic powder; place the ribeye steak in the Cook & Crisp Basket. 3. Put on the Smart Lid on top of the Ninja Foodi Steam Fryer. 4. Move the Lid Slider to the "Air Fry/Stovetop". Select the "Air Fry" mode for cooking. 5. Cook the ribeye steak at 200°C for around 15 minutes, turning it over halfway through the cooking time. 6. Top the ribeye steak with the cheese and serve warm. Serve.

Per serving: Calories: 399; Fat:29.4g; Carbs: 4.6g; Fibre: 0.3g; Sugars: 0.7g; Proteins: 29.2g

Savoury Rump Roast

⏲ **Prep Time: 10 minutes** 🍲 **Cook: 50 minutes** ❖ **Serves: 4**

680g rump roast
Black pepper and salt, to taste
1 teaspoon paprika
2 tablespoons olive oil
60ml brandy
2 tablespoons cold butter

1. Place the Cook & Crisp Basket in your Pressure Cooker Steam Fryer. 2. Brush the basket with oil. 3. Toss the rump roast with the black pepper, salt, paprika, olive oil, and brandy; place the rump roast in Cook & Crisp Basket. 4. Put on the Smart Lid on top of the Ninja Foodi Steam Fryer. 5. Move the Lid Slider to the "Air Fry/Stovetop". Select the "Air Fry" mode for cooking. 6. Cook the rump roast at 200°C for around 50 minutes, turning it over halfway through the cooking time. 7. Serve with the cold butter and enjoy!

Per serving: Calories: 390; Fat:22.4g; Carbs: 1.4g; Fibre: 0.4g; Sugars: 0.6g; Proteins: 35.2g;

| Chapter 6 Beef, Pork, and Lamb

Chapter 7 Desserts

62 Chocolate Chip Cookies
62 Egg Custard
63 Zesty Raspberry Muffins
63 Butter Cake
64 Peach Crumble
64 Chocolate Mug Cake
65 Sugared Dough Dippers with Chocolate Sauce
65 Nutty Fruitcake
66 Molten Lava Cake
66 Pumpkin Pudding

Chocolate Chip Cookies

⏰ **Prep Time: 10 minutes** 🍲 **Cook: 30 minutes** ⬨ **Serves: 8**

85g sugar
115g butter
1 tablespoon honey
170g flour
1 ½ tablespoon milk
55g chocolate chips

1. Place the Cook & Crisp Basket in your Pressure Cooker Steam Fryer. 2. Mix the sugar and butter using an electric mixer, until a fluffy texture is achieved. 3. Stir in the remaining ingredients, minus the chocolate chips. 4. Gradually fold in the chocolate chips. 5. Spoon equal portions of the mixture onto a lined baking sheet and flatten out each one with a spoon. Ensure the cookies are not touching. 6. Place in the Cook & Crisp Basket. Put on the Smart Lid on top of the Ninja Foodi Steam Fryer. Move the Lid Slider to the "Air Fry/Stovetop". Select the "Air Fry" mode for cooking. Adjust the cooking temperature to 175°C. 7. Cook for around 18 minutes.

Per serving: Calories 148; Fat: 0.7g; Sodium 3mg; Carbs: 57.4g; Fibre: 5.1g; Sugars 40.4g; Protein 2g

Egg Custard

⏰ **Prep Time: 25 minutes** 🍲 **Cook: 10 minutes** ⬨ **Serves: 6**

6 big eggs, beaten
150g sugar
A pinch of salt
1 tsp. vanilla extract
960ml milk
360ml water
¼ tsp. cinnamon

1. Whisk the eggs, sugar, salt, vanilla, and milk in a bowl until combined. 2. Pour the mixture into six ramekins and cover with foil. 3. Poke some holes in the foil. 4. Pour the water into the pot and place in the rack. Place the ramekins on the rack. 5. Close the lid, turn the pressure release valve to SEAL position, and then move the slider to PRESSURE. Select HI and set the cooking time to 7 minutes. Press START/STOP to begin cooking. When finished, release the pressure naturally. 6. Remove the ramekins from the pot and let them cool for 3 minutes. 7. Sprinkle the dish with cinnamon and serve.

Per Serving: Calories 213; Fat: 9.51g; Sodium: 160mg; Carbs: 20.75g; Fibre: 0.1g; Sugar: 20.69g; Protein: 10.66g

| Chapter 7 Desserts

Zesty Raspberry Muffins

⏲ Prep Time: 10 minutes 🍳 Cook: 35 minutes 🍽 Serves: 10

1 egg
250g frozen raspberries, coated with some flour
360g flour s
100g sugar
160ml vegetable oil
2 teaspoon baking powder
Yoghurt, as needed
1 teaspoon lemon zest
2 tablespoon lemon juice
Pinch of sea salt

1. Place the Cook & Crisp Basket in your Pressure Cooker Steam Fryer. 2. Place all of the dry recipe ingredients in a bowl and mix well. 3. Beat the egg and pour it into a cup. Mix it with the oil and lemon juice. Add in the yoghurt, to taste. 4. Mix the dry and wet recipe ingredients. 5. Add in the lemon zest and raspberries. 6. Coat the insides of 10 muffin tins with a little butter. 7. Spoon an equal amount of the mixture into each muffin tin. 8. Transfer to the Cook & Crisp Basket. Put on the Smart Lid on top of the Ninja Foodi Steam Fryer. Move the Lid Slider to the "Air Fry/Stovetop". Select the "Air Fry" mode for cooking. Adjust the cooking temperature to 175°C. 9. Cook for around 10 minutes, in batches if necessary.

Per serving: Calories 257; Fat: 16.5g; Sodium 1031mg; Carbs: 23.6g; Fibre: 3.4g; Sugars 6.1g; Protein 4.7g

Butter Cake

⏲ Prep Time: 10 minutes 🍳 Cook: 25 minutes 🍽 Serves: 2

1 egg
180g flour
7 tablespoon butter, at room temperature
6 tablespoon milk
6 tablespoon sugar
Pinch of sea salt
Cooking spray
Dusting of sugar to serve

1. Place the Cook & Crisp Basket in your Pressure Cooker Steam Fryer. 2. Spritz the inside of a suitable ring cake tin with cooking spray. 3. In a suitable bowl, mix the butter and sugar using a whisk. 4. Stir in the egg and continue to mix everything until the mixture is smooth and fluffy. 5. Pour the flour through a sieve into the bowl. 6. Pour in the milk, before adding a pinch of salt, and mix once again to incorporate everything well. 7. Pour the prepared batter into the tin and use the back of a spoon to made sure the surface is even. 8. Place in the Cook & Crisp Basket. Put on the Smart Lid on top of the Ninja Foodi Steam Fryer. Move the Lid Slider to the "Air Fry/Stovetop". Select the "Air Fry" mode for cooking. Adjust the cooking temperature to 180°C. 9. Cook for around 15 minutes. 10. Before taking it out of the Pressure Cooker Steam Fryer, check that the cake is fully cooked by inserting a toothpick into the centre; it should come out clean. Allow the cake to cool, then serve it dusted with sugar.

Per serving: Calories 281; Fat: 6.7g; Sodium 187mg; Carbs: 52.7g; Fibre: 6.6g; Sugars 29g; Protein 5.1g

Chapter 7 Desserts | 63

Peach Crumble

⏱ **Prep Time: 10 minutes**　🍲 **Cook: 35 minutes**　📚 **Serves: 6**

680g peaches, peeled and chopped
2 tablespoon lemon juice
120g flour
1 tablespoon water
100g sugar
5 tablespoons cold butter
Pinch of sea salt

1. Place the Cook & Crisp Basket in your Pressure Cooker Steam Fryer. 2. Mash the peaches a little with a fork to achieve a lumpy consistency. 3. Add in two tablespoons of sugar and the lemon juice. 4. In a bowl, mix the flour, salt, and sugar. Throw in a tablespoon of water before adding in the cold butter, mixing until crumbly. 5. Grease the Cook & Crisp Basket and arrange the berries at the bottom. Top with the crumbs. 6. Put on the Smart Lid on top of the Ninja Foodi Steam Fryer. Move the Lid Slider to the "Air Fry/Stovetop". Select the "Air Fry" mode for cooking. Air Fry for around 20 minutes at 200°C.

Per serving: Calories 363; Fat: 10.7g; Sodium 253mg; Carbs: 63.7g; Fibre: 3.8g; Sugars 22.9g; Protein 4.9g

Chocolate Mug Cake

⏱ **Prep Time: 10 minutes**　🍲 **Cook: 15 minutes**　📚 **Serves: 1**

1 tablespoon cocoa powder
3 tablespoon coconut oil
30g flour
3 tablespoons whole milk
5 tablespoon sugar

1. Place the Cook & Crisp Basket in your Pressure Cooker Steam Fryer. 2. In a suitable bowl, stir all of the recipe ingredients to mix them completely. 3. Take a short, stout mug and pour the mixture into it. 4. Put the mug in your Ninja Foodi Pressure Steam Fryer. Put on the Smart Lid on top of the Ninja Foodi Steam Fryer. Move the Lid Slider to the "Air Fry/Stovetop". Select the "Air Fry" mode for cooking. Cook for around 10 minutes at 200°C. You can drizzle with some chocolate sauce if desired.

Per serving: Calories 361; Fat: 31.3g; Sodium 385mg; Carbs: 13.8g; Fibre: 7.3g; Sugars 2.5g; Protein 9.7g

Sugared Dough Dippers with Chocolate Sauce

⏱ **Prep Time: 10 minutes**   🍲 **Cook: 45 minutes**   🍽 **Serves: 5**

150g sugar
455g friendly bread dough
240g heavy cream
340g high quality semi-sweet chocolate chips
115g butter, melted
2 tablespoon extract

1. Place the Cook & Crisp Basket in your Pressure Cooker Steam Fryer. 2. Coat the inside of the basket with a little melted butter. 3. Halve and roll up the prepared dough to create two 15-inch logs. Slice each log into 20 disks. 4. Halve each disk and twist it 3 or 4 times. 5. Lay out a cookie sheet and lay the twisted dough pieces on top. Brush the pieces with some more melted butter and sprinkle on the sugar. 6. Place the sheet in the Cook & Crisp Basket. Put on the Smart Lid on top of the Ninja Foodi Steam Fryer. Move the Lid Slider to the "Air Fry/Stovetop". Select the "Air Fry" mode for cooking. 7. Adjust the cooking temperature to 175°C. 8. Air Fry for around 5 minutes. Flip the prepared dough twists over, and brush the other side with more butter. Cook for an additional 3 minutes. It may be necessary to complete this step in batches. 9. In the meantime, make the chocolate sauce. Firstly, put the heavy cream into a suitable saucepan over the medium heat and allow it to simmer. 10. Put the chocolate chips into a large bowl and add the simmering cream on top. Mix the chocolate chips everything until a smooth consistency is achieved. Stir in 2 tablespoons of extract. 11. Transfer the fried cookies in a shallow dish, pour over the rest of the melted butter and sprinkle on the sugar. 12. Drizzle on the chocolate sauce before serving.

Per serving: Calories 469; Fat: 36.5g; Sodium 46mg; Carbs: 31.4g; Fibre: 4.5g; Sugars 17.9g; Protein 9.1g

Nutty Fruitcake

⏱ **Prep Time: 15 minutes**   🍲 **Cook: 20 minutes**   🍽 **Serves: 8**

1 (230g) can crushed pineapple, including juice
75g raisins
80g dried unsweetened cherries
80g pitted and diced dates
60g pecan halves
60g chopped walnuts
30g unsweetened coconut flakes
100g sugar
55g melted butter, cooled
2 teaspoons vanilla extract
2 tablespoons fresh orange juice
4 large eggs
120g all-purpose flour
2 teaspoons baking powder
¼ teaspoon salt
¼ teaspoon ground nutmeg
240ml water

1. Combine all ingredients except water in a medium bowl. Grease a cake pan, and press mixture into the pan. 2. Pour 240ml water into the pot and place in the rack. Lower the pan onto rack. 3. Close the lid, turn the pressure release valve to SEAL position, and then move the slider to PRESSURE. Select HI and set the cooking time to 20 minutes. Press START/STOP to begin cooking. When finished, release the pressure naturally. 4. Transfer the pan to a cooling rack. Refrigerate the cake covered overnight. 5. Flip onto a cutting board, slice, and serve.

Per Serving: Calories 735; Fat: 22.25g; Sodium: 179mg; Carbs: 128.68g; Fibre: 4.9g; Sugar: 110.46g; Protein: 10.06g

Molten Lava Cake

⏰ **Prep Time: 25 minutes**   🍲 **Cook: 10 minutes**   ❖ **Serves: 1-2**

480ml water
1 egg, beaten
1 tsp. vanilla extract
120g semi-sweet chocolate chips
4 tbsp. butter, soft
2 tbsp. flour
45g powdered sugar

1. Grease the ramekin with butter. 2. Whisk the egg and vanilla in a small bowl. 3. Melt the chocolate with butter in a saucepan over medium heat, and then let the mixture cool for about 30 seconds. 4. Add the egg mix, flour and sugar to the chocolate mixture, stir them to combine. 5. Fill the ramekin halfway-full. 6. Pour the water into the pot and place in the rack. Place the ramekin on the rack. 7. Close the lid, turn the pressure release valve to SEAL position, and then move the slider to PRESSURE. Select HI and set the cooking time to 7 minutess. Press START/STOP to begin cooking. When finished, release the pressure naturally. 8. Serve and enjoy.

Per Serving: Calories 423; Fat: 32.79g; Sodium: 241mg; Carbs: 27.79g; Fibre: 1g; Sugar: 20.17g; Protein: 6.09g

Pumpkin Pudding

⏰ **Prep Time: 10 minutes**   🍲 **Cook: 25 minutes**   ❖ **Serves: 4**

720g pumpkin puree
3 tablespoon honey
1 tablespoon ginger
1 tablespoon cinnamon
1 teaspoon clove
1 teaspoon nutmeg
240g full-fat: cream
2 eggs
240g

1. Place the Cook & Crisp Basket in your Pressure Cooker Steam Fryer. 2. In a suitable bowl, stir all of the recipe ingredients to mix. 3. Grease inside of the Cook & Crisp Basket. 4. Pour the mixture into the Cook & Crisp Basket. 5. Put on the Smart Lid on top of the Ninja Foodi Steam Fryer. 6. Move the Lid Slider to the "Air Fry/Stovetop". Select the "Air Fry" mode for cooking. 7. Adjust the cooking temperature to 200°C. 8. Cook for around 15 minutes. Serve with whipped cream if desired.

Per serving: Calories 360; Fat: 7.8g; Sodium 280mg; Carbs: 74.4g; Fibre: 8g; Sugars 47.4g; Protein 2.7g

Chapter 7 Desserts